A Steam Odyssey

A Steam Odyssey

The Railroad Photographs of Victor Hand

With an Introduction by Don Phillips
Afterword by Jeff Brouws

Edited by Wendy Burton

W. W. Norton & Company
New York   London

A Steam Odyssey:
The Railroad Photographs of Victor Hand

Copyright © 2013 by Victor Hand
Introduction © 2013 by Don Phillips
Afterword © 2013 by Jeff Brouws
All rights reserved
Printed in Italy
First Edition

Book design and composition by Jeff Brouws
Editing and sequencing by Wendy Burton

Manufacturing by Elcograf S.p.A

Library of Congress Cataloging-in-Publication Data
Hand, Victor.
    A Steam odyssey : the railroad photographs of Victor Hand /
introduction by Don Phillips ; afterword by Jeff Brouws.—First edition.
    pages cm
ISBN 978-0-393-08431-3 (hardcover)
1. Railroads—Pictorial works. 2. Steam locomotives—Pictorial works.
3. Photography of railroads. 4. Hand, Victor. I. Phillips, Don, 1942- II. Title.
 TF149.H28 2013
 625.26'1—dc23
                        2013009408

(previous page)
PLATE 1 Western Maryland Scenic Railroad
2-8-0 734 eastbound at Helmstetter's Curve,
Maryland, 2003

Additional photographs:
PAGE 7 Pennsylvania Railroad 4-4-2 7002
and 4-4-0 1223 crossing the Susquehanna River
at Rockville, Pennsylvania, 1985

PAGE 21 Turkish State Railways 2-10-0 56724
with a westbound freight train at Gumus, 1973

PAGE 189 Southern Railway excursion train
crossing the Ashley River at Charleston,
South Carolina, 1970

This book is dedicated to my wife, Patricia, and my daughters, Emily and Katherine, who have been tolerant of my constant traveling and proud of my photography.

Introduction

Two Million Miles in Pursuit of Steam:
The Railroad Photographs of Victor Hand

Don Phillips

VICTOR HAND IS A DETERMINED, talented perfectionist who has spent most of his life photographing railroads, working for railroads, helping save railroads from bankruptcy and ruin, and seeing much of the world from trackside. For close to six decades Hand's passion for steam has resulted in a body of work covering locomotives and the railroad environment over six continents and some fifty countries. His photographs reflect in some ways the straightforward, no-nonsense nature of his personality. The compositions are strong and forceful. He captures the power and grandeur of steam locomotives over and over again. There is, however, another aspect to his photography that becomes apparent after spending time studying his work: his appreciation for and lyrical presentation of the widely varying landscapes the railroads traverse. Landforms shaped the railroad and, conversely, railroads transformed the land. This aspect of his work is the greatest revelation his negatives have to offer.

In carefully archived and preserved 4 x 5–inch glassine envelopes, Victor has stored the images of almost every major railroad in the United States and more than fifty countries. Along the way he has been arrested, deported, gored by a bull, lost several cars to a grade-crossing crash or traffic accident, and lived an adventure that cannot be duplicated. For some of those out-of-the-way places where steam disappeared long ago, his negatives are the only quality images ever recorded. Some of the countries don't even exist any more.

For the first eighteen years of his life, Hand's educational track seemed to follow his father's plan that he become a doctor, but there were early signs a career in medicine was not what Victor himself wanted. This became a point of friction between father and son. For a time, Hand went along with his self-assured father's wishes, though eventually he left his premed studies to pursue a law degree. He graduated from the New York University School of Law in May 1966. The evening of his last exam he boarded a plane to Japan to begin what would

become a worldwide search for the steam engine. Returning in November 1966, he spent a month chasing the legendary *Phoebe Snow* streamliner on the Erie-Lackawanna Railroad before it was discontinued. The day he finished the bar exam, in early 1967, memories of Victorian Railways' massive Hudson engines propelled him out of the country once again, this time to photograph trains in Australia and New Zealand. He was admitted to the New York State Bar in May 1967, while still on the road, but he made no attempt to enter a law practice. Although he gained admittance to the bar his interest was the railroad.

HAND'S PHOTOGRAPHIC STYLE WAS FORGED in the crucible of *Trains* magazine in the 1950s, Lucius Beebe's *The Age of Steam*, and the works of Dick Kindig, Henry Griffiths, Walter Thrall, Robert Hale, and O. Winston Link. "These men had a profound influence on my photography, and they still do," he says. He traces his love of steam to *Trains* and a series of articles written by then editor David P. Morgan and illustrated by the photographer Philip Hastings called "Steam in Indian Summer." Morgan wrote and Hastings photographed with excitement and love, telling the story of tracking down the last of U.S. and Canadian steam as it rapidly succumbed to the diesel. Morgan's wonderful prose hooked our generation on this type of locomotive power. For more than five decades since then, a small fraternity of railroad enthusiasts has scoured the world for steam, which survived much longer in China, Africa, South America, Asia, and the Soviet Union and its eastern European satellites than in the United States and Canada. Hand was a pioneer among his contemporaries in the pursuit of foreign steam. His relentless drive to photograph these engines after their demise in the United States propelled him thousands of miles away from home at a time when this simply was not being done by others.

American rail enthusiasts in those days were notorious for turning up their noses at railroading anywhere outside North America, but Hand had an ally in Morgan, who began to travel the world looking for steam in the early 1960s. In fact, when Morgan began hunting through his files for foreign steam images, almost the only quality shots belonged to Hand and the British photographer George F. Heiron. On page 38 of the April 1963 issue of *Trains* magazine appeared Hand's very first magazine shot—a four-cylinder Castle-class 4-6-0 at Paddington Station in London, just arrived with an express on the day after Christmas 1961 (page 170, plate 128). Hand's foreign steam shots immediately began gracing the pages of *Trains*, and in the April 1966 issue he was the featured photographer for a Morgan piece on South Africa with the headline "Finally, a Photographer Equal to the Occasion." His records indicate that he has had 124 photos in *Trains*.

Those of us who were old enough to photograph mainline steam before its demise in the spring of 1960 did not even think of foreign steam when we first began our lifetime chase. The United States and Canada were the first hunting grounds for Hand and our kind, and the Norfolk and Western was the promised land, the last U.S. railroad to cast its lot with steam. In the late 1950s Roanoke, the headquarters city for N&W, was filled with it. The N&W stretched across mountain ranges from Cincinnati to Norfolk, and its locomotives were huge. The Blue Ridge grade just east of Roanoke was the center of the drama, with heavy coal trains blasting regularly up the grade with a sound that attacked the ears and the heart. Passenger trains rated beautiful streamlined J-class locomotives capable of 100 mph–plus speeds in places where the curves allowed, mainly crossing the Great Dismal Swamp headed for Norfolk. N&W steam began disappearing by 1957, but as late as the spring of 1960 it was possible to find patches of it in the West Virginia hills and hollows. When Victor and I first set foot on sacred ground in 1958, the N&W was still the holy grail of steam. Although we had not yet met, it now seems inevitable that our paths would cross.

YOUNG VICTOR HAD HEARD about the N&W and wanted to travel from New York to Roanoke in time to catch the big show. But he was only fifteen in early 1958, so his mother volunteered to go with him. Family friends traveling from New York to Florida drove them to the N&W passenger station in Suffolk, Virginia, near Norfolk, to catch a train to Roanoke. Hand remembers his disappointment as the train pulled into the station. He mistook the streamlined J-class 4-8-4 steam engine, first built during World War II and fitted after the war with a

beautiful bulletnose streamlined shroud, for a diesel. He soon learned it was not. The N&W was a wonderfully hospitable railroad for railway enthusiasts in those days, and the conductor spent time talking to the Hands as the train roared toward Roanoke. Unbeknownst to Victor, the conductor had called ahead to headquarters to let them know a young railfan was on the way.

On the platform to greet the Hands as they stepped from the train in Roanoke was a Norfolk and Western public relations man. He had set up tours of the N&W's steam shops and the Shaffers Crossing yards and steam servicing facilities for the next few days. In the shops, Hand remembers, was no. 600, the original J, getting its last major overhaul. This handful of remarkable days left an indelible impression on the boy and may well have galvanized his lifelong passion for railroading.

That first Roanoke trip with his mother was the beginning of an intense three-year search for the remaining pockets of steam in the United States and Canada. In addition to N&W, several other major railroads still had at least some steam operations as the 1950s drew to a close, and Hand saw and photographed most of them—the Canadian Pacific, Canadian National, Grand Trunk Western, Illinois Central, and Duluth, Missabe and Iron Range. He missed Union Pacific steam by a month in the middle of 1959, finding numerous UP locomotives stored at Cheyenne, Wyoming, some of the boilers still a little warm.

Victor and I met in November 1958 at Boaz siding near Vinton, Virginia, where Y6 pushers were staged to help coal trains to the top of the Blue Ridge grade. I had arranged to ride a pusher, which turned out to be Y6 no. 2157, assigned to help a heavy coal train over the summit. Hand had hitched a ride to Roanoke from a slightly

Norfolk and Western Railway 4-8-4 611 at Eckman, West Virginia, 1982

FIGURE 2 Norfolk and Western Railway Y-6 2-8-8-2 pushes a coal train up the Blue Ridge grade at Vinton, Virginia, 1958

older military friend, Don Wilson. We met when Hand walked up to "pusher siding" to take a photo of the big locomotive as it sat, thumping and wheezing, awaiting its next assignment. We've never forgotten that meeting. It was probably the last time a very strong-minded Victor Hand ever took my photo advice. Another pusher came rolling down the mountain from its assignment and Victor walked in front of the 2157 to shoot the other engine. "Hey kid," I said. "Come back here and get the low-pressure cylinder in the shot." It was a wonderfully nice photo, with the 2157's big forward cylinder in the foreground and the other Y6 descending the grade in the background. We hit it off and have been traveling together for more than five decades since then (figure 2 at right).

Victor and I later spent two weeks around New Year's 1959–60 photographing steam in French Canada in deep snow. That included spending several hours on New Year's Eve aboard a steam-powered mixed train of one coach and several freight cars on our way to Megantic, Quebec. The coach was crammed full, bottles were emptied, and the air was filled with laughter and Canadian French. The locomotive headlight played off snowbound pine trees, and the melodious whistle punctuated the air (page 152, plate 114). At the end of our Canadian trip a few days later, I casually mentioned to him that I would send return postcards to any roundhouse in the United States that might possibly still have steam. We knew that the N&W and the Grand Trunk Western were still running a few of these engines, and both Canadian roads had small pockets of them, but we thought steam was dead on the rest of the major railroads. The first few return postcards seemed to confirm that.

Then what felt like the miraculous occurred. A postcard from the foreman at the Illinois Central's Paducah, Kentucky, roundhouse told us that steam had arisen from the grave there, at least briefly. Twelve engines had been pulled from the dead line to help handle a traffic surge—four big 2-10-2s, four 4-8-2s, and four 0-8-0 switchers. One call to Hand and we set plans to get to Paducah as soon as possible. This small railroad town located at the confluence of the Ohio and Tennessee Rivers was a wonderful surprise, and we spent as much time as possible there between February and April, when the new 9400-class diesels arrived and steam went back to the dead line for the last time. April 1960, in fact, turned out to be the last sigh of mainline steam in all of North America. Numerous short lines continued to operate those engines for many years but it just wasn't the same. Those like Hand and I who had seen big-time steam wanted to see more, but how?

Slowly it became clear to Victor that the rest of the world was still filled with steam. "When steam disappeared in this country, and really, I missed most of it, I discovered Mexico," he said in a 2006 interview in *Trains* magazine. After the United States and Canada went diesel in 1960, Hand said he had seriously considered giving up railroad photography. "But two things had happened. I became interested in diesels, and I saw George F. Heiron's photos of English steam. Like O. Winston Link's photos in the 50s, that got my interest. Then I discovered South Africa and hammered away at steam there for the next decade."

Hand's first trip to South Africa came in 1965, followed by numerous return trips over the years. South Africa was a mecca for steam, with 2,663 locomotives in service when he arrived, and Hand was perhaps the first non–South African rail enthusiast to visit the country. Several trips later, in 1968, he ran into Charlie Lewis, a South African Railways employee who was a rail enthusiast and excellent photographer. That meeting began another lifelong friendship and gave Victor a local source who knew the country's best photo spots and where the trains were running. South Africa was slow to dieselize its operations because it had abundant coal but no oil. As a pariah state at that time because of its racial separation policies, South Africa did not dare depend on any other country for oil, so it developed a policy of slowly electrifying main lines while steam handled most of the country's traffic for decades, well into the 1980s.

In 1971 I took my first of what would be many overseas journeys with Victor. Every trip was an adventure in some way. We learned how the world worked. We absorbed different cultures. We froze on Manchurian hillsides in February. We marveled at roiling oceans. We discovered the awesome beauty of South Africa's Cape Province in April. We visited a thousand places that tourists never see. We argued politics in the world's hot spots. We watched wonderful countries such as Zimbabwe deteriorate into chaos. We saw South Africa arise from apartheid. We survived on gruel and we ate wonderful food in high-class restaurants. We fought malaria. We learned to be alert for lions and gangs of baboons. And we learned that railroaders everywhere are pretty much the same.

BACK IN 1967, AFTER HE'D ENDED his halfhearted attempt at becoming a lawyer, Hand began an odyssey that became a recurring cycle of working for a railroad for a year or so, getting laid off, traveling the world in search of steam, and then hiring on with another railroad. He has been immensely fortunate in that his lifelong passion for photographing the railroad dovetailed with his long and varied career in the

rail industry. His interest in the physical plant of railroading informed his photography and continues to do so.

His first railroad job was in August 1967 as a fireman on the New York Central at Rochester, New York, a mixture of yard switching assignments and road freight jobs. Laid off after a year, he took a few photos before landing a job as a switchman at the Erie-Lackawanna's rat-infested Croxton yard at Secaucus, New Jersey.

Hand had always wanted to get into railroad management, a quest that was not easy and almost didn't happen. Five railroads turned down his application to join their management-training programs, and the Penn Central didn't even answer his letter. His railroading career seemed moribund, but sometimes things happen for odd reasons. Victor wrote an article for *Trains* on the Penn Central's Empire Service passenger trains in New York State. That article caught the attention of Mike Weinman, who was then involved with the Penn Central's management training program. Weinman talked to Gordon Fuller, the head of the program, who agreed to talk to Hand. He was offered a job by the end of the interview.

The training program provided more drama than planned. He entered it in 1969, in time for a big eastern blizzard. However, just before he graduated from the program in early 1970, the East was hit with an even more vicious blizzard, the worst in many years. Freights were stranded everywhere and some were called lost. Even train crews could not remember where they had left trains to seek shelter in whiteout conditions. Some consists were almost buried beneath snowdrifts, and all trainees were ordered into the blizzard to do anything they could to help keep the railroad running. Hand reported to the railroad's Operating Department and one of his first assignments was to find a lost 104-car coal train.

His first full-time job after the training program was as an assistant trainmaster—the lowest management rank in the Operating Department—at Newberry Junction near Williamsport, Pennsylvania. Those were nasty days on the Penn Central. Labor seemed to hate management with a passion and never wasted time in showing its contempt. Hand had no way of knowing, but his first big challenge at Penn Central, the 1970 blizzard, had been the final straw in the company's life as a private enterprise. Its horrid finances became a disaster as the blizzard sapped the last strength from what was already a hopeless dream. Even as Hand fought to keep freight moving at Newberry Junction into the spring of 1970, Penn Central's end was near. The railroad's chairman Stuart Saunders and its finance manager David Bevan had managed to hide Penn Central's true condition

A pair of QJs take a westbound China Rail freight train up the grade at Sha Pi Tou, 1993

through a fog of confusing paperwork. Difficult as it is to believe today, the White House and Congress had almost no idea that the largest bankruptcy in U.S. history, to that date, was only weeks away. Penn Central's top management obfuscated through month after month of sinking finances until they could no longer do so.

On Sunday, June 21, 1970, just 873 days after Penn Central was formed, Hand was on duty at Newberry Junction when the word came that the railroad's lawyers had paid a morning visit to Judge C. William Craft Jr. at his home to file bankruptcy papers. It was soon time for Hand to move on. Six months later he resigned and headed west to look for work, but neither Southern Pacific nor Western Pacific was hiring, so he left on an exhaustive yearlong, round-the-world photo trip. He traveled to Japan, France, Germany, Austria, Czechoslovakia, Kenya, Tanzania, Rhodesia, South Africa, Indonesia, Malaysia, Thailand, Singapore, and Argentina.

The year 1971 proved to be an enormously productive and educational photographic period for Victor. He traveled and made photographs for twelve solid months. He was able to explore new places as well as return to countries where he had previously just scratched the surface. Hand spent three full months taking photographs in South Africa, and tremendous satisfaction came from the experience of investigating the railroads there in such depth. This year, too, would be the last opportunity Hand had for such extensive traveling. After this time his career became much more demanding and he had the great good fortune of meeting Patricia, his future wife.

Returning to the United States and looking for work again, Hand's luck held up. His friend Gordon Fuller had left Penn Central and hired on at Jersey Central as general superintendent. Fuller immediately hired Victor as manager of passenger services. Conflicts with top management caused him to leave a year later. He took a step backward and became a brakeman on Penn Central's Northeast Corridor in late 1972. However, a new path to railroad management had opened by then, and Hand jumped at the chance to take it. Amtrak had been formed on May 1, 1971, to take over most of the country's passenger trains, and the skeletal organization was badly in need of experienced railroaders. Amtrak hired Hand in 1973 as a marketing analyst, and one of his first tasks was to plan utilization of Amtrak's first major passenger car order, 492 new cars from the Budd Company, called Amfleet cars. These are the now familiar tubular cars that are ubiquitous on the Northeast Corridor's short-distance routes and on single-level long-distance routes in the East.

Victor, however, wanted to get back into train operations. He made two applications, one to Amtrak's service department and another to the new U.S. Railway Association, which was formed in 1974 to redraw the map of bankrupt eastern railroading—the Penn Central, the Erie-Lackawanna, the Jersey Central, the Lehigh Valley, the Ann Arbor, the Reading, and the Lehigh and Hudson River. The resulting railroad was to become Conrail, a slimmed-down amalgam of the best main lines and branches of all the bankrupt lines. He was immediately accepted for both jobs. He picked the USRA, perhaps the most important professional decision of his life. By the dozens, the best and the brightest of railroading and government flocked to the USRA. They had no promise of a job after their task was completed. They were not bureaucrats but risk takers, exactly the kind of people needed, and Hand had all the skills necessary to do the job. He was put in charge of developing an operating plan for Conrail and picking which main lines and yards would survive—decisions that have had a lasting impact on the face of North American railroading to this day.

In the 1970s, railroads were still tightly regulated by the Interstate Commerce Commission. Not a single line could be abandoned, not a passenger train could be discontinued, nor any freight rate or service changed except by ICC approval. That whole regulatory system came unraveled when Congress created Amtrak and then the USRA. Deregulation was the order of the day in all forms of transportation. In 1971, the Federal Railroad Administration was given the sole jurisdiction to decide which passenger trains to abandon, and Congress gave the USRA even more power. The USRA had the singular authority to decide which main lines and branches to abandon. Congress basically transferred to the USRA all congressional powers to take any action needed to form Conrail. At the very end, Congress could reject the final system plan, but no one even pretended that legislators would take such drastic action because that would almost surely throw the entire eastern railroad system into chaos. Congress would then be forced to nationalize the private railroad system, too terrible a decision for the government to take, economically or politically.

The job of Hand and his small staff was to choose the facilities that would be folded into Conrail. He also supervised the property conveyance process, which became the largest real estate transaction in U.S. history. As it turned out, his railroad photography was a critical part of the skill set he brought to the task. He had an almost photographic memory of the map of eastern railroading and has walked much of it with his cameras. He had the final decision on matters that could profoundly affect eastern real estate values. If the USRA

said a line was needed for Conrail, that decision was final no matter how much anyone objected. The bankruptcy trustees of the various railroads could protest all they wanted. After all, some urban land had a huge value for nonrailroad purposes, but very little of it was being obtained for Conrail on the basis of its value as a going concern for railroad purposes. The government would pay pennies on the dollar for land taken for Conrail compared to huge amounts the trustees would receive for urban land Conrail didn't need. Others in the USRA handled a job that was considered more politically sensitive: to pick the branch lines that would be abandoned unless states or local governments decided to subsidize them. But Hand's group managed the high-stakes transactions.

The USRA experience was challenging. During the big push at the end of its final planning, USRA people worked day and night up to sixteen hours a day including weekends. Starting in the early winter of 1975 Hand worked five months straight, seven days a week, including Thanksgiving, Christmas, and New Year's. On his first day off, he drove to Pennsylvania to take pictures of the Lehigh Valley, which would soon be absorbed into Conrail.

Victor Hand emerged from the USRA with a reputation that made him a valuable commodity. He was hired by a major consulting firm beginning in 1977 to work on railroad projects. In the next two decades Hand assisted on projects for all the major North American railroads, government agencies, and railroads in South America, Europe, Africa, Australia, and the former Soviet Union. It was ideal work that blended his professional straights with his photographic calling. In 1988 he became an independent consultant as he began slowly to ramp down his professional career. However, that career came full circle in the late 1990s when Norfolk Southern hired him as a consultant to help split Conrail between NS and CSX, taking apart the very railroad he had played a major part in putting together twenty-three years earlier. He and his colleagues had done such a masterful job putting Conrail together that it drew the unbelievable price of $10 billion when it was divided.

IN 1992, HAND BOUGHT PROPERTY on the rocky Maine shore near Bar Harbor and built a house on the foundations of an old mansion. In 2000 he and his wife, Patricia, along with their two daughters, Emily and Katherine, left Washington, D.C., and moved to their new home in Maine. His basement became the site of a huge model railroad layout of the New York Central Hudson and Electric Divisions around Harmon, New York, as the railroad would have appeared in 1948–1951.

His research was extensive, searching out old photos and maps and doing many on-site excursions. He approaches this layout with the same precision and drive for perfection that he has always manifested in both his professional and his photographic lives.

Victor Hand's railroad excursions have never ended. In 1980 he made one of the first rail photography trips to China, although he had little opportunity to take action photographs. The Chinese tour guides insisted on structured tours and meetings with officials. On later trips into the 1990s and 2000s, the China International Travel Service gradually learned that rail photographers wanted to take photos of trains, not dancing children, and life was a little easier on the road. Finally, China allowed private guides to lead tours, and several guides grew quite professional at finding photo locations. A photograph of two China Rail freight trains meeting at Sha Pi Tou siding taken in 1993 (page 82, plate 53) is one of many that are included in this volume.

Hand traveled to the Soviet Union for the first time in 1990. Russia and its satellite states had thousands of remaining steam locomotives because even after full dieselization and electrification the military insisted on keeping "strategic dumps" of steam locomotives around the country in case of war. Some of those locomotives were available for private rail enthusiast trips when the Soviet Union fell. For almost a decade, it was possible to organize excursion trains in the former Soviet republics of Ukraine, Belarus, and Russia that were pulled by different steam locomotives every day and could stop almost anywhere for photos. Hand and his friend David Goodheart arranged a ten-day tour in February 1994 pulled by matched double-headed steam locomotives every day, mostly in the snow. Double-headed Soviet Railways SO-17-class 2-10-0s at Malinitci, Ukraine, taken in 1994 (page 25, plate 4), is one of many examples of work from this time.

FIGURE 3 Southern Pacific Daylight 4-8-4 rolls eastbound with Mount Shasta in the background, at Macdoel, California, 1981

Union Pacific Railroad 4-8-4 8444 runs through frigid weather conditions at Winifred, Kansas, 1985

FIGURE 4 Canadian Pacific
Royal Hudson 2839
on Southern Railway at
Orange, Virginia, 1979

French National Railways
passenger locomotives on the
ready track at Le Mans, 1964

Victor is a resolute man and it shows in his photography. He knows exactly what kind of photographs he wants and settles for nothing less. He may be the only rail enthusiast still using a 4 x 5 Speed Graphic, last made in 1965. His photos are crystal clear and usually in perfect light. He does not consider himself an artist but there is beauty in his artistry. He says he wants clear and sharp photos with absolutely no distractions, not a single weed showing above the rail, and no human being other than railroad crew members are allowed in the frame. The photo must be well lighted, either by the sun or by flashbulbs. His set of criteria has served him well for over five decades and these principles are not likely to change in the future. He has logged some two million miles in pursuit of his passion, and that number will continue to grow in years to come.

Hand never tires of telling the story of his father, who was determined that his son become a doctor. In the decade between his trip to Roanoke with his mother and his final decision to abandon law as a profession, Hand's father encouraged his hobby, even giving him a Rolleiflex camera to take photos of trains. His busy father never traveled with him on photo excursions, and the realization that his son had totally lost interest in law came to him slowly. The shock of trading law for a (then) failing industry was difficult for his father to accept, but Hand believes he later came to understand the wisdom of his son's decision. The body of work that Victor has contributed to the canon of railroad photography is inspiring. His energetic pursuit of steam railroading around the world had an enormous impact on railroad photography in the United States, breaking through an invisible border and paving the way for other railroad photographers to leave the confines of North America and seek steam abroad. He led the way with his characteristic fervor and made the railroading world a bigger and more interesting place for all of us.

Photographs
1958–2009

PLATE 2 Mexicano Railway 2-8-0 212 and
NdeM 2-8-2 2113 prepare to leave Apizaco,
Tlaxcala, with a "Directo" freight train
for Mexico City, 1962

PLATE 3 Nevada Northern Railway 4-6-0 40 with a mixed train at Hiline, Nevada, 1992

PLATE 4 Double-headed Soviet Railways SO-17-class 2-10-0s at Malinitci, Ukraine, 1994

PLATE 5 Soo Line 4-6-2 with a passenger train
crossing the St. Croix River at Cedar Bend,
near Osceola, Wisconsin, 1998

PLATE 6 British Railways Britannia 4-6-2
at the engine terminal in Rugby, England, 1963

PLATE 7 Canadian Pacific Railway 4-6-4 2816
westbound at Massive, Alberta, 2006

PLATE 8 British Railways goods train
bound for Perth at Forteviot, Scotland, 1964

PLATE 9 National Railways of Mexico
4-8-4 3045 works upgrade through a
thunderstorm at Bernal, Querétaro, 1964

PLATE 10 French National Railways Pacific 231.G 285
from atop the coaling tower at Le Mans, France, 1964

PLATE 11 Management and train crew confer on the
station platform at Le Havre, France, 1964

PLATE 12 South African Railways 19D-class
4-8-2 2692 approaches the Lootsberg Pass at
Blouwater, Cape Province, 1992

PLATE 13 Interior view of Eastleigh Locomotive Works
on British Railways' Southern Region, 1964

PLATE 14 Japanese National Railways 4-6-4 C62-24 starts
a local passenger train north out of Taira, Honshū, 1966

PLATE 15 Inspection pits at South African Railways'
Beaconsfield locomotive shed in Kimberley, Cape Province, 1965

PLATE 16 Union Pacific Railroad 4-8-4 8444
lays over at Oakley, Kansas, 1986

PLATE 17 Two mixed trains meet on the Devil's Nose switchbacks on
the Guayaquil and Quito Railway near Sibambe, Ecuador, 1996

PLATE 18 Guayaquil and Quito Railway 2-8-0 53 climbs the upper
level of the switchbacks on the Devil's Nose near Sibambe, Ecuador, 2003

PLATE 19 Pennsylvania Railroad 4-4-2 7002 and 4-4-0 1223 crossing the Susquehanna River at Rockville, Pennsylvania, 1985

PLATE 20 Atchison, Topeka and Santa Fe Railway
4-8-4 3751 on the Grand Canyon Railway
at Willaha, Arizona, 2002

PLATE 21 Mexicano Railway 2-8-0 210
in the roundhouse at Apizaco, Tlaxcala, 1962

PLATE 22 British Railways 5015 "Kingswear Castle"
at speed on the Western Region main line, 1961

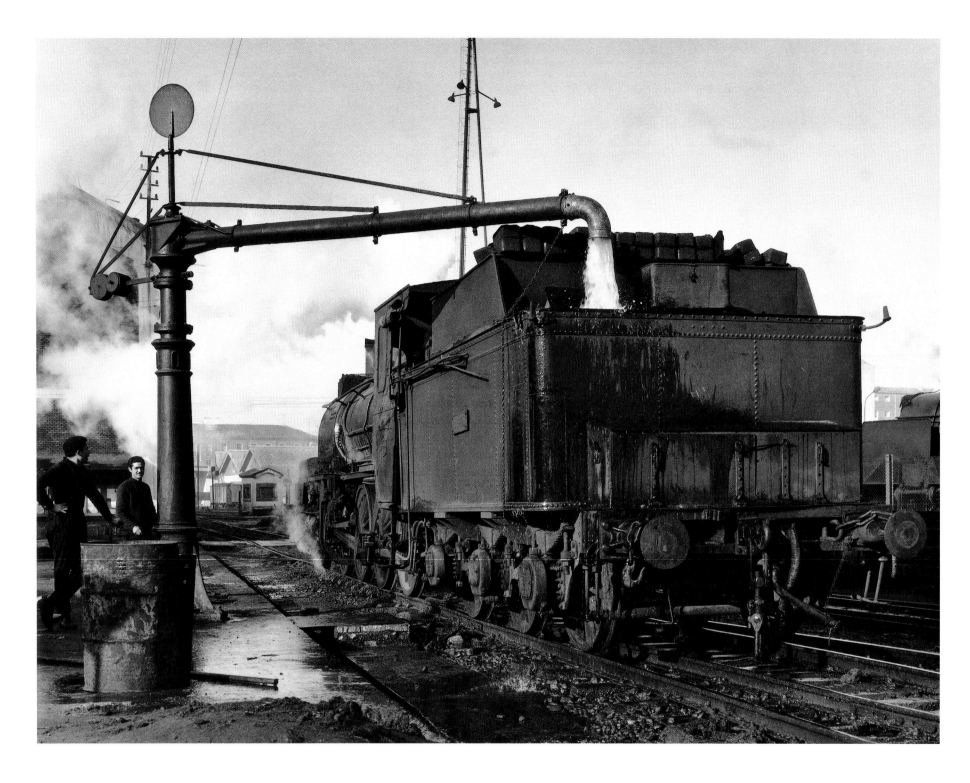

PLATE 24 Spanish National Railways 2-8-0 takes water
at the locomotive depot at Valladolid, 1965

PLATE 25 A laborer cleans the fire on South African Railways
GD 2-6-2+2-6-2 Garratt 2231 at Alicedale, Cape Province, 1965

PLATE 26 Japanese National Railways
C-61-class 4-6-4 starts a passenger train out
of Ikarigaseki, Honshū, in a blizzard, 1971

PLATE 27 Northbound South African Railways freight train ascends the Lootsberg Pass after a heavy snowfall, 1971

PLATE 28 Three ex–Chicago and North Western 2-8-0s are readied for night runs on National Railways of Mexico at Tierra Blanca, Veracruz, 1962

PLATE 29 New Zealand Government Railways class J 4-8-2 1237 at the station in Greymouth, South Island, 1967

PLATE 30 Freight train passing Denver and Rio Grande Western water tank at Cresco, Colorado, 1967

PLATE 31 Western Maryland Scenic Railroad 2-8-0 734 entering Brush Tunnel on the former Western Maryland Railway Connellsville line in Maryland, 2003

PLATE 32 British Railways A-1-class Pacific 60147
"North Eastern" at Edinburgh, Scotland, 1962

PLATE 33 British Railways locomotives
on the ready tracks at York, England, 1963

PLATE 34 Turkish State Railways 2-10-0 56724
with a westbound freight train at Gumus, 1973

PLATE 35 Anshan Iron and Steel Company blast furnaces are serviced by an SY 2-8-2, Anshan, China, 1995

PLATE 36 Grand Trunk Western Railroad 4-8-4 6319 at Pontiac, Michigan, after hauling a commuter train from Detroit, 1959

PLATE 37 Mississippian Railway 2-8-0 77
with a freight train at Smithville, Mississippi, 1986

PLATE 38 Irún–Madrid express on the
Spanish National Railways at Pancorbo, Spain, 1965

PLATE 39 15E-class 4-8-2s rest at South African Railways Bethlehem locomotive shed in the Orange Free State, 1965

PLATE 40 Norfolk and Western Railway class A westbound at Bluefield, West Virginia, 1987

PLATE 41 Two South African Railways GEA-class 4-8-2+2-8-4 Garratts are under the coal dock at Greyville locomotive shed in Durban, Natal, 1965

PLATE 42 British Railways 7026 "Tenby Castle" leaving Wolverhampton, England, 1962

PLATE 43 Spanish National Railways
roundhouse at Soria, 1965

PLATE 44 Union Pacific Railroad 4-6-6-4 3985 lays a thick trail of smoke across the plains at Wyoming, Wyoming, 1982

PLATE 45 Four French National Railways 2-8-2s in the locomotive depot at Le Mans, 1963

PLATE 46 Buffalo Creek & Gauley Railroad hopper train at Avoca, West Virginia, 1963

PLATE 47 Maclear branch passenger train eastbound on South African Railways at Glen Wallace, Cape Province, 1971

PLATE 48 British Railways engine driver on the foot plate of Britannia Pacific 70041 "Sir John Moore," running on the former Great Central Railway main line, 1963

PLATE 49 Drive wheels and rods of Union Pacific Railroad 4-8-4 8444 at Cheyenne, Wyoming, 1968

PLATE 50 Ferrocarriles Argentinos
double-headed mixed train near Lepá, 1991

PLATE 51 Helper locomotive on Denver and Rio Grande Western pipe train at Los Pinos, Colorado, 1967

PLATE 52 Denver and Rio Grande Western Railroad freight train, Los Pinos, Colorado, 1967

PLATE 53 China Rail freight trains
meet at dusk at Sha Pi Tou siding, 1993

PLATE 54 Nickel Plate Road 2-8-4 759
at the Erie-Lackawanna Railroad terminal
at Hoboken, New Jersey, 1969

PLATE 55 Milwaukee Road 4-8-4 261
in the fog at Gouldsboro, Pennsylvania, 1996

PLATE 56 China Rail westbound freight
leaves a deep cut on the grade at
Meng Jia Wan, 1993

PLATE 57 Belgrano Railway 2-10-2 1354
crosses the Viaducto Polvorillo west of
San Antonio de los Cobres, Argentina, 1972

PLATE 58 Duluth, Missabe & Iron Range Railway 2-8-8-4 under the coal dock at Proctor, Minnesota, 1961

PLATE 59 Illinois Central Railroad 4-8-2 2524 at Paducah, Kentucky, 1960

PLATE 60 Westbound mixed train runs downhill on the Guayaquil and Quito Railway at Siberia, Ecuador, 2003

PLATE 61 South African Railways 19D-class 4-8-2 with a westbound special passenger train on the Maclear branch at Glen Wallace, Cape Province, 1992

PLATE 62 Norfolk and Western Railway 4-8-4 611 at Plum Run, Ohio, 1992

PLATE 63 Triple action shot on
South African Railways at Bloemfontein,
Orange Free State, 1971

PLATE 64 American-built Liberation 2-8-2s at the French National Railways Nevers roundhouse, 1968

PLATE 65 Soviet Railways SU-class 2-6-2 in a blizzard at Matarov, Ukraine, 1992

PLATE 66 Mozambique Railways 4-8-2
on the turntable at Lourenço Marques,
Mozambique, 1966

PLATE 67 German Federal Railways class 44
2-10-0 leaves Kassel, West Germany, 1964

PLATE 68 A mechanic tightens a pipe joint on a South African Railways locomotive at Bethlehem, Orange Free State, 1965

PLATE 69 French National Railways 4-8-2 241.P17 at the Le Mans engine terminal, 1963

PLATE 70 Southern Pacific and Union Pacific 4-8-4s ascend Cajon Pass on parallel tracks at Alray, California, 1989

PLATE 71 Southbound South African Railways freight train at Toorwater, Cape Province, 1975

PLATE 73 Indonesian State Railways
local passenger train at Tjitjapar, Java, 1971

PLATE 74 Rebuilt Merchant Navy–class 4-6-2
35003 "Royal Mail" at Basingstoke, England, 1961

PLATE 75 Double-headed C-62-class Hudsons on Japanese National Railways at Shikaribetsu, Hokkaidō, 1971

PLATE 76 Black Five 4-6-0s pass on
British Railways at Carlisle, England, 1964

PLATE 77 Three British Railways 2-6-0s
around the indoor turntable at
York, England, 1963

PLATE 78   Southbound National Railways of Mexico freight train near Victor Rosales, Zacatecas, 1962

PLATE 80 New Zealand Government Railways 4-8-4 climbing Cass Bank, South Island, 1966

PLATE 81 Nickel Plate Road 2-8-4 759 westbound on Penn Central near Horseshoe Curve, Pennsylvania, 1970

PLATE 82 Indonesian State Railways
mixed train on the high bridge at
Lebakdjero, Java, 1971

PLATE 83 Western Maryland Scenic Railroad
2-8-0 734 westbound at Helmstetter's Curve,
Maryland, 2003

PLATE 84 French National Railways Pacific 231.E 624 at Montluçon, 1968

PLATE 85 Soviet Railways class SU passenger locomotive at Kolevka, Ukraine, 1994

121

PLATE 86 Pere Marquette Railway 2-8-4
1225 rests at Carland, Michigan, 2007

PLATE 87 Nickel Plate Road Berkshire
765 at Henderson, Michigan, 2009

PLATE 88 Chesapeake and
Ohio Railway 4-8-4 614 passes
the water column at Quinnimont,
West Virginia, 1985

PLATE 89 Canadian Pacific
Railway 4-4-0 29 at St. Lin,
Quebec, 1960

PLATE 90 Spanish National Railways
240F 2586 entering the tunnel
at Torralba, Spain, 1965

PLATE 91 German Federal Railways local
passenger train crosses the Rhine River at
Köln, West Germany, 1964

PLATE 92 Union Pacific Railroad 4-8-4 8444
eastbound at Bitter Creek, Wyoming, 1968

PLATE 93 Canadian National Railways
4-8-4 6218 at Shanty Bay, Ontario, 1967

PLATE 94 Denver and Rio Grande Western
rotary snowplow at Lobato, New Mexico, 1993

PLATE 95 Fireman wets down the coal on New Zealand Government Railways 4-8-2 1232 at Greymouth, South Island, 1967

PLATE 96 South Australian Railways 4-8-4 523 at Mile End locomotive shed in Adelaide, South Australia, 1966

PLATE 97 Canadian National Railways
4-8-4 6218 at Glanford, Ontario, 1965

PLATE 98 Soo Line 2-8-2 1003 and 4-6-2
2719 in the rain at Osceola, Wisconsin, 1998

PLATE 99 Victorian Railways R-class 4-6-4
at Ararat, Victoria, Australia, 1966

PLATE 100 British Railways 35029 "Ellerman Lines" with a
London Waterloo–Yeovil express at Basingstoke, England, 1961

PLATE 101 A QJ 2-10-2 heads a China
Rail passenger train at Shi Nao, 1995

PLATE 102 South African Railways passenger
train westbound on the Bethlehem–Bloemfontein
line at Meynell, Orange Free State, 1992

PLATE 103 German Federal Railways
freight train crossing the Mosel River at
Bullay, West Germany, 1971

PLATE 104 A French National Railways suburban train leaves Gare St-Lazare in Paris, 1964

PLATE 105 Medina del Campo station on Spanish National Railways, 1965

PLATE 106 Running shed staff prepare Rhodesia Railways 15A-class Garratt 420 for service at Bulawayo, Rhodesia, 1966

PLATE 107 Coronation 4-6-2 46225 "Duchess of Gloucester" on British Railways at Carlisle, England, 1964

PLATE 108 British Railways A-4 Pacific 60010 "Dominion of Canada" at Perth, Scotland, 1964

PLATE 109 An Aberdeen–Manchester fish train pulled by a Britannia 4-6-2 prepares to leave Perth, Scotland, 1964

PLATE 110 Norfolk and Western Railway 4-8-4 611 on the bridge westbound at Coopers, West Virginia, 1982

PLATE 111 New Zealand Government Railways goods train crossing the Waimakariri River on the South Island, 1966

PLATE 112 Ferrocarriles Argentinos
narrow-gauge passenger train at
Aguada Troncoso, 1991

PLATE 113 Double-headed goods train on
New South Wales Government Railways near
Amaroo, New South Wales, Australia, 1967

PLATE 114 Canadian Pacific Railway
D-10-class 4-6-0 under the coal dock at
Vallée Jonction, Quebec, 1959

PLATE 115 Savannah & Atlanta Railway
4-6-2 750 at speed on Seaboard Air Line
Railroad tracks near Statham, Georgia, 1966

PLATE 117 British Railways goods train with a banking engine on the rear climbing to Shap summit, at Scout Green, England, 1964

PLATE 118 Japanese National Railways
D52-404 southbound along the Hokkaidō
coast at Rebun, 1971

PLATE 119 St. Louis–San Francisco Railway
4-8-2 1522 northbound on Wisconsin Central
Ltd. rails at Grayslake, Illinois, 1988

PLATE 120 Chicago, Burlington & Quincy Railroad
2-8-2 4960 at Ashburn, Missouri, 1966

PLATE 121 Pusher Locomotive on Denver and Rio Grande Western Railroad narrow-gauge freight train, Lobato, New Mexico, 1965

PLATE 122 National Railways of Mexico Niagra 4-8-4 with northbound freight train at San Juan del Río, Querétaro, 1964

PLATE 123 South African Railways GB-class Garratt on the Barkly East branch in Cape Province, 1992

PLATE 124 Japanese National Railways D-52 2-8-2 with a southbound freight train at Ōnuma, Hokkaidō, 1966

PLATE 125 Cuyahoga Valley Scenic Railroad
2-8-2 4070 eastbound on the Pittsburgh & Lake
Erie Railroad at Pittsburgh, Pennsylvania, 1975

PLATE 126 Union Pacific Railroad 4-6-6-4
3985 climbs Sherman Hill in a blizzard
at Lynch, Wyoming, 1984

PLATE 127 Union Pacific Railroad
2-8-0 618 along Deer Creek Reservoir
at Decker Bay, Utah, 2002

PLATE 128 British Railways Castle 4-6-0 at the bumping blocks in Paddington Station, London, 1961

PLATE 129 Niagra 3054 backs out of National Railways of Mexico's roundhouse at the Valle de Mexico terminal, 1964

PLATE 130 British Railways interregional passenger train leaves Basingstoke, England, 1961

PLATE 131 British Railways goods train with a banking locomotive leaves the yard at Beattock, Scotland, 1964

PLATE 132 Downgrade freight
train on Denver and Rio Grande
Western Railroad, Los Pinos,
Colorado, 1965

PLATE 133 Alberta Prairie Railway
2-8-0 41 at Big Valley, Alberta, 2006

PLATE 134 Guatemalan Railways 2-8-0 at Los Encuentros, Guatemala, 1977

PLATE 135 Pakistan Railways passenger train climbs the Khyber Pass at Ali Masjid, 1994

PLATE 136 Eastbound freight train on Denver and Rio Grande Western Railroad at Los Pinos, Colorado, 1965

PLATE 137 Soviet Railways freight train in the snow at Malinitci, Ukraine, 1994

PLATE 140 South African Railways
15E-class 4-8-2 2939 awaits an
evening departure from Bethlehem,
Orange Free State, 1965

PLATE 141 National Railways of
Colombia 2-8-0 at Bogotá, 1966

PLATE 142 British Railways luxury train
"The Queen of Scots" leaves Edinburgh
Waverley Station for London, 1962

PLATE 143 An ancient shop engine rides
the turntable at the Spanish National Railways
locomotive depot at Valladolid, 1965

PLATE 144 Denver & Rio Grande Western narrow-gauge locomotives 487 and 483 lay over at Chama, New Mexico, engine house, 1965

Photographer's Notes

Victor Hand

Southern Pacific Daylight 4-8-4
4449 below Mount Shasta at
Black Butte, California, 1992

I HAVE ALWAYS CONSIDERED MYSELF a railway enthusiast rather than a photographer. I like to see big steam locomotives working hard, and I turned to photography as a way to preserve the memories of some of the wonderful engines I have seen.

I never had any formal training in photography, learning by trial and error and with the help of a few special friends who shared my interest in railways. My father was an accomplished amateur photographer and he gave me a Rolleiflex to use in my early teenage years. Unfortunately, he had no time to go out on the railroad and show me how to take pictures, but he did set up a darkroom for me, gave me basic instructions, and critiqued my early work.

The Rolleiflex had an excellent lens, but it took me a while to work out the intricacies of exposure, shutter speed, and depth of focus. I saw some wonderful railroad sights in the late 1950s, but my early photographic efforts were crude at best. Steam locomotives were disappearing fast in the United States at this time, and I soon learned from the railroad magazines that many railroads were operating excursion trains with their remaining steam locomotives. I went on a number of these trips and discovered that there were many who shared my interest. I spoke to a lot of different people, and I learned where steam was still operating. A few of the younger railroad enthusiasts that I met became friends and we started traveling together to see the last of steam. Several of these friends were of great assistance to me in learning how to take good railroad pictures.

Ronald Wright and I met on an excursion train during the 1958 convention of the National Railway Historical Society in Toronto. Although he was my age, Ronald was well ahead of me on the photographic learning curve. He had traveled in the western New York area with some experienced railroad photographers, and he shared his knowledge and helped me improve my composition and exposure skills. Ronald also got me in the habit of keeping careful notes of what I had photographed, and these notes have proved to be most useful in preparing this book more than fifty years later.

Ronald introduced me to Gordon Roth, who was a commercial photographer trained at the Rochester Institute of Technology. Gordon was among a group who perfected the art of railroad action photography using large-format cameras in the 1940s. He persuaded me to buy a 4 x 5–inch Speed Graphic camera. We made a number of trips to Colorado to photograph the Denver and Rio Grande Western Railroad's narrow-gauge steam operations in their last few years, and on the long drives from the east coast to Colorado Gordon would talk photography and I would soak up the information like a sponge. Gordon suggested I read Ansel Adams's five-volume text on photography. Adams, the renowned landscape photographer, was the leading technical expert on the subject. I had to read these books several times before I understood what he was saying, but they provided valuable guidance on composition, optics, lighting, exposure, chemistry, and other technical aspects of photography.

During these years I learned that several things were necessary to make good railroad photographs. You need the correct equipment and the know-how to use it; you need to have a vision of the kind of photographs you want to produce; you need to be in the right spot at the right time; and you need the determination and stamina to put up with the difficulties of getting to the right spot.

THE CORRECT EQUIPMENT FOR ME turned out to be a 4 x 5 Speed Graphic with a focal plane shutter. The lenses that were supplied with these cameras were not optimal for railroad photography, but I acquired five superb lenses made by Voigtländer and Schneider, which have served me well. The 1/1000 of a second focal plane shutter solved the problem of stopping the motion of fast-moving trains. The weak point in a Speed Graphic is the front standard that holds the lens. If it is manhandled or knocked a tedious realignment is necessary to restore the optics, and I soon learned to check this in the ground glass on a regular basis. The benefit of the design of the front standard on these cameras is that it allows the photographer to raise the lens to keep vertical lines parallel, which is extremely handy when buildings or railroad structures such as signals or catenary are in the compostion. The 4 x 5 film had to be loaded into film holders, which was often a daunting task in the field, and it took some time for me to figure out how to

keep dust out of the holders (blow out the light traps with compressed air and load film in a swabbed-down hotel bathroom). My traveling companions soon learned to put up with my film changing and to stay clear of the front standard.

I found that it was critical to standardize my use of film types, exposure, and development times. Film manufacturers changed their film quite often over the years, and each time this happened I had to make carefully controlled tests of the old and the new films or developers to determine for myself optimum results.

In 1971 I was planning a trip to Indonesia, and as car rentals were unavailable in that country I needed to travel light. For this trip I purchased a Pentax 6 x 7 cm single-lens reflex, which used 120 roll film, and stashed my large-format equipment in a hotel in Singapore for two months. The 6 x 7 did a fine job and I continue to use that format from time to time.

Western Maryland Scenic Railroad 2-8-0 734 eastbound at Georges Creek Junction, Maryland, 2003

I ACQUIRED AN IDEA OF THE KIND of photographs I wanted to produce by examining the work of others. I began reading *Trains* magazine in the mid-1950s and absorbed the work of Phil Hastings, Dick Steinheimer, Jim Shaughnessy, Stan Kistler, David Plowden, and Frank Barry. In 1957 my mother bought me a copy of Lucius Beebe's masterpiece *The Age of Steam,* which contained the work of many other notable photographers, including Robert Hale, Dick Kindig, Bill Middleton, Walter Thrall, and Henry R. Griffiths Jr. These people took the kinds of pictures I wanted to take, and I studied their work.

Jim Shaughnessy's well-known night photo of Canadian National Railway's 6173 at St. Albans, Vermont, opened my eyes to the potential of night photography. In 1958 someone from the Norfolk and Western Railway sent me a copy of a booklet entitled *Night Trick* on the Norfolk and Western, which contained a sample of O. Winston Link's night action photography, and soon I began experimenting with large flashbulbs. I never was able to set up the kind of complex shots that Link made but I did build a capacitor-discharge unit that would dependably fire four or five flashbulbs—and I was on my way. Carrying this equipment on airplanes proved to be difficult, and I often took a simplified (and lighter) set of night equipment on overseas trips.

Although I was interested in the mechanical details of the locomotives I saw, I soon concentrated my efforts on action photography out on the line. This involved searching out scenic locations, and often a number of attempts were required to get a picture right, given all of the variables of lighting, weather, wind, and locomotive smoke. Luck often played a big part in making a successful shot. Sometimes

you could be following a train and just stumble into an outstanding location. Of course, I didn't neglect the chance to take engine pictures when I could, and locomotive sheds and roundhouses presented many opportunities for interesting photography.

Locomotive roster photography is a specialty that became popular among railroad photographers in North America in the 1930s and '40s. A classic roster shot is more than just a side view of a locomotive. The setting must be perfect, with a clear foreground and no poles, buildings, or other obstructions behind the engine. The sunlight must be low three-quarter front, the drive rods must be spotted in the lowest quarter, the engine must be fairly clean, and steam leaks and smoke must be eliminated.

My good friend and traveling companion Harold Edmonson knew several of the old-time roster photographers who lived around Chicago, including Walter Krawiec and Charles Felstead. Harold and I were traveling together in southern Africa in 1966 and decided to try and set up roster shots where the opportunity presented itself. There were plenty of good locations for this, and the sunlight always cooperated during the African winter. On one memorable afternoon in Bloemfontein, South African Railways locomotive foreman Gert Coetzee assigned two hostlers to move engines for the visiting photographers. In two hours they moved one of every class of engine on the shed to the selected spot and posed them with rods down (right).

IN ORDER TO BE IN THE RIGHT SPOT at the right time you have to do your homework. The first problem was to find out where steam engines were in use. In the United States and Canada the decline of steam operations was well documented in *Trains* magazine and the other railroad publications, and there was lots of information to be gleaned from the grapevine as well when I met other enthusiasts on excursion trains. An "official guide" was necessary to see where the tracks went and to plan trips by rail. As steam disappeared in the United States and Canada, I began to seek out steam operations in other countries. Articles in magazines showed me the potential in Mexico, where many U.S.-built or secondhand American locomotives still ran.

David P. Morgan, the editor of *Trains,* published a portfolio of the work of the British photographer George F. Heiron. I liked the look of British engines and soon went to investigate. There was an abundance of information in the British railway periodicals about which engines were running where, and I devoured it all. A British publication called *Continental Railways* provided tips on where to go in Europe, and the newsletter *World Steam* contained brief reports

from intrepid British steam enthusiasts from the far corners of the world.

In 1963 I noticed a picture of a South African Railways 4-8-4 condensing locomotive in *Trains* magazine, taken by C. P. Lewis. Unable to find out much about South African Railways in my usual source, *Jane's World Railways*, I visited the South African consulate in New York. The consul knew nothing about the country's railroads, but he did have a railway annual report that, among the financial information, listed 2,663 steam locomotives by wheel arrangement. I wrote a letter to the general manager in Johannesburg asking some questions and received a four-page single-spaced reply from the assistant to the general manager, who was a railway enthusiast named Barclay. He told me what was running, and where the busy lines and heavy grades were. Barclay said that the general manager, Mr. Rezelman, wanted to meet me when I visited, since I was one of the first overseas photographers to come to South Africa. Mr. Rezelman proved to be very interested in my journey and provided letters of introduction that allowed me access to all South African Railways facilities.

Jane's World Railways was a reference book published in England with details of most of the railways in the world. *Jane's* was often out of date, as I discovered on my first trip around the world. When I landed on the Indian Ocean island of Mauritius I found the railway had been abandoned several years earlier and all that remained

was one coach and a locomotive steam dome in the weeds. The next plane out was four days later, and my traveling companion Harold Edmonson and I had a few days of rest and recreation on a very interesting tropical island before we continued on to South Africa.

Jane's supplied the names and addresses of railway officials and I always wrote ahead for letters of introduction or photographic permits. Things were pretty free and easy in North America back in the 1950s and '60s, and local supervisors would usually grant permission to visit roundhouses and yards. Crews were, in general, also welcoming, and locomotive cab rides were easy to come by. Overseas, however, was another story. Even in Great Britain the railways were wary of trespassers and photo permits were necessary. In European countries such as France and Germany just after the war railway staff were frequently suspicious. In Franco's Spain and Salazar's Portugal the police were downright paranoid about strangers photographing railways.

I avoided the eastern European countries while they were under communist governments. On a foray near East Germany's border with West Germany to photograph Deutsche Reichsbahn engines where they crossed into the West I was picked up by the local police. The Berlin Wall had just gone up and tensions were high. The authorities called the U.S. Army base nearby and I wasted a nice sunny day talking to a CIA agent, who was very interested in my notebooks. He advised me to leave Germany and not photograph any more "railheads," as he called them. I told him I would continue to do what I was doing and went about my business. Perhaps the CIA still has my name in its files.

A friend had managed to ride across the Trans-Siberian Railway in the early 1970s, and he even took a few photographs along the way, but his stories put me off. This same friend later photographed railways in East Germany and ended up spending six months as a guest of the government until the appropriate bribes were paid to get him out. After the breakup of the Soviet Union and the demise of the communist governments in Europe, I made many trips to that part of the world and obtained some pleasing photographs.

Once I arrived at a railway that operated steam locomotives it was necessary to find photo locations. Topographic maps, railway timetables, and track profiles were useful in this task, but in the end lots of scouting and poking around were the surest ways to determine where the best spots lay on a particular line. Sometimes other railway enthusiasts provided guidance. As an example, my South African friend Charlie Lewis had photographed trains all over his country and he steered me to dozens of spectacular locations that I probably would not have found on my own.

Weather conditions played an important part in planning a trip, and in the pre-Internet days it was not so easy to find weather information. I relied for the most part on a booklet published by Pan American World Airways, which gave data on average rainfall, temperature, and hours of sunshine per month in various cities around the world.

AS A YOUNG MAN I HAD PLENTY of determination to see as much steam as I could, as well as the stamina to put up with the heat, cold, filth, bugs, poor food, and the other hardships of travel in third world countries. This is not to say that all of my trips involved hardship. Europe of course was a very civilized place to travel in those days, as was southern Africa, Australia, and New Zealand. Japan, Southeast Asia, and South America were reasonably comfortable places to travel when I stayed in the cities, but rural areas offered more of a challenge. Travel conditions in China were primitive in the early days but, as the economy developed, accommodations for travelers improved, although again rural areas were always difficult.

I visited India for a week in 1966 and took a few pictures. After seeing conditions in that country, and knowing the Indians were still building steam locomotives, I decided to leave that country for last. I never managed to get back. India is the one that got away.

Often the best conditions for photographing steam locomotives were in the winter, and in places such as Canada, northern China, and northern Japan the winter temperatures can be brutal. Proper equipment and lots of determination were required to photograph under these conditions, but the results were often exceptional. I will admit to a sense of relief when China finished operating mainline steam in regular service in 2005 (the last place in the world to do so), for I will not now be tempted to go to northern China again in winter.

The end of regular service mainline steam operations in the United States and Canada to the last steam operations in China took forty-five years. During that time I traveled overseas as much as I could. Plenty of time was available while I was in school, with Christmas and spring breaks and three-month summer vacations. Once I started my railroad career time became more of a problem, and later on family obligations sometimes took precedence. Even when I didn't have big blocks of time to travel overseas I kept busy on shorter trips and on weekends photographing numerous North American steam excursions that still operated, in addition to photographing electric and diesel-powered trains in the United States and Canada.

As the years passed mainline steam excursions became fewer, and the trains were not as pleasing to photograph because of the use of mismatched equipment and extra water tenders. A number of short line railroads and preservation groups owned steam locomotives, and so it became possible for groups of photographers to charter trains. A lot of work goes into organizing these photographic charter trains, including dealing with the operating railroad, locating authentic equipment, and repainting locomotives and cars. My friends John Craft, David Goodheart, and Dave Gross enjoyed doing this work and set up many memorable charter trips, which yielded some excellent photographs.

Railway photography for me has proven to be an all-consuming interest that has dominated and enriched my life. I have traveled to many places not seen by the average tourist, and I have seen how people in other countries live. Along the way I have made many good friends. My railroad interest also led to a very satisfying, long career in the railroad industry.

As I have gotten older I find that I enjoy going out on photographic expeditions as much to see friends as to take photographs.

Double-headed Soviet Railways P-36-class 4-8-4s at Krasnoselka, Ukraine, 1994

Victor Hand, Roger Spotswood, Harold Edmonson, and Charlie Lewis waiting for a train, Viaducto Polvorillo, Argentina, 1972 (page 87, plate 57)

David Goodheart and Victor Hand enjoy a laugh on a railway platform, Poland, 1972 (Photo by Bob Avery)

195

Afterword

Jeff Brouws

I OWE VICTOR HAND AN APOLOGY. As a young rail enthusiast, provincial Californian, and someone weaned on the images of Richard Steinheimer and his left coast acolytes, I wasn't paying much attention to train photography from other parts of the United States. The only prominent East Coast railroad photographer I knew by name was Jim Shaughnessy. Nor had I yet cultivated any interest in foreign railroads. Steam locomotives of French descent or Russian design—with their strange, otherworldly shapes—looked alien to my American eyes. Unfortunately, these blind spots of geography and industrial culture made it all too easy to overlook the fine photography being done by Hand that appeared regularly in *Trains* magazine during the late 1960s and throughout the 1970s. I'm pleased that these oversights can now be righted with the publication of *A Steam Odyssey*. This book I believe will give further voice to the importance of Hand's fifty-year contribution to the field of railroad photography.

AS I'VE AGED MY THINKING has become more inclusive. Youthful nearsightedness has given way to more expansive viewpoints. As a result of my friendship with Ed Delvers beginning in the early 1980s, my attitude about railroads and railroad photography beyond American borders began to shift. Through his extensive book and magazine collections, Ed shared his planetary perspective about trains, a perspective he came by honestly. Ed was born in Los Angeles and moved to Japan at age two, where he lived until his late teens. This relocation gave him an eclectic character: he had no trouble adoring simultaneously Japanese National Railways' raven-black C-62 4-6-4 steam engines, Shay locomotives operating on logging roads in Taiwan, or PCC cars running through the streets of San Francisco. Under his tutelage my prejudice about foreign railroading dissolved. Trains had a universal appeal and could be enjoyed wherever they ran. And steam was steam. Engines looked different from country to country and they all had an intriguing unfamiliarity that deserved further exploration.

Of the many railroad books and magazines Ed put before me, one man's photography and name popped up repeatedly: Victor Hand. Bold double-page spreads in *Japan Railfan* magazine or razor-sharp pictures appearing in well-printed foreign and domestic publications with Victor's byline underneath were too numerous to count. Ed and I were always engaged in friendly argument over the artistic merits of one railroad photographer versus another but it was clear Hand was near the top of his list. Thanks to this edification, Hand was rapidly climbing mine too.

I also mention Delvers here because he became an important contact for Victor Hand during Hand's first trip to Japan in 1966. Ed liked to connect one group of people with another; he was a goodwill ambassador of the first magnitude. Selflessly he arranged a meeting between Hand and Kentaro Hirai, Kenichi Matsumoto, and Takao Takada—two prominent Japanese railfan publishers and a venerated steam locomotive designer. They acted as virtual tour guides, giving Hand (and pal Harold Edmonson) directions to many in-country locations for railroad photography that otherwise might have eluded them. Of the many surprises I've encountered while working on *A Steam Odyssey* these past two years was the heretofore unknown connection Victor and I shared with Ed, who passed away tragically nine years ago. Ed would have delighted in seeing this volume of Victor's finest work come to fruition. I'm glad he encouraged me to take a deeper look thirty years ago.

Another aside related to Victor: around 1981 Delvers and I started working on a book project that would eventually be published in 2000 as *Starlight on the Rails*. In gathering material for that book we had the good fortune to receive a box of splendidly made 11 x 14s by Hand. The technical skill with which these pictures were crafted was remarkable and decidedly old school: single-weight, fiber-based, ferrotyped prints that were tonally immaculate, with crisp highlights and plenty of mid-tone and shadow detail. And keep in mind these were night photographs, which made their tonalities all the more noteworthy. Their extreme clarity and sharpness were not only the result of Hand's 4 x 5 camera and the Schneider and Voigtländer lenses he used, but also the product of his technical proficiency—from correctly exposing the image to the developing of the film to the making of the print. They were the most perfect black-and-white prints I'd ever handled.

In retrospect, it was only our fear of including too much foreign material in a book essentially made for the American market that kept us from using more of his work. Perhaps a prudent decision at the time but one I now regret. This is all to say that this box of photographs further awakened me to Hand's mastery. (A postscript to this story: inexplicably this batch of pictures was never returned to Victor and the photographs lay misplaced in my files for eleven years, only to be unearthed in 2011 to become the basis for *Odyssey*. Lucky for us all.)

ALTHOUGH INITIALLY I MAY HAVE overlooked Victor's foreign imagery as seen in *Trains*, some of his stateside pictures appearing in that publication did sink in. One photograph in particular, of a Rio Grande narrow-gauge freight train crossing a high alpine valley in Colorado (see *Trains*, January 1967, and page 178, plate 136 here), stopped me in my tracks. Its striking aesthetics of a diminutive train enveloped by an expansive landscape, surrounded by the punctuating darker contrasts of trees dotting the mountainside, made for a compelling composition. This image, incidentally, echoes the work of the nineteenth-century landscape photographer William Henry Jackson, who was well known for his Colorado "views" of trains. Hand, like Jackson before him, is enthralled with the bold geographies that railroads run through worldwide and likes to use trains as a scale device to show off the immensity and grandeur of the land. Therefore it's no accident that Hand's Colorado imagery, and much of his foreign work, bears a striking resemblance to Jackson's in its ability to capture deep pictorial space, its veneration of nature, its emphasis on scenic qualities, and its precise large-format description of technological achievement, in other words photos capturing the railroad tracks themselves as an earthwork defining, shaping, altering, and moving through the landscape.

If one could put together two men who had been alive in different epochs, I would have no trouble at all envisioning Jackson and his tripod-mounted mammoth-plate camera standing alongside Victor and his companions as they collectively marvel at the radical engineering of the Devil's Nose, while recording the train's slow ascent up switchbacks on the Guayaquil and Quito Railway in Ecuador (see pp. 40–41, plates 17 and 18). It will be remembered, by the way, that Jackson, under contract to the World's Transportation Commission, traveled extensively across the globe between 1894 and 1896 shooting railways and their physical plants (stations, bridges, viaducts, loops, and switchbacks) in innumerable foreign countries, many places Victor also would eventually travel to. Even though a century separates the

lives of these two photographers their kinship is unmistakable, so similar are their aesthetic intentions and desires for the kinds of photographs they liked to make. [1]

ANOTHER REASON I HADN'T PAID attention to Victor's work earlier is because when younger I was dismissive of the three-quarter perspective in train photography, of which Hand is a dedicated practitioner. Photographers working in this style weren't on my radar—it all seemed too easy to me (which it isn't). However, over the past decade, as I delved into the technical finesse required to make such images and began to understand the importance of the style itself within the overall historic development of American railroad photography, my eyes opened. I learned that rail historians such as John H. White and George Hilton thought the three-quarter view the single best depiction of railroading ever devised. Being able to deeply immerse myself in Hand's body of work over the course of the two-year *Odyssey* project has given me a renewed respect for this opinion and the genre. However, though Hand's approach to rail photography is firmly rooted within the three-quarter tradition, his photography is so much more than that. Let's call it second-generation three-quarter school taken to the next level, a hybrid style utilizing the concepts of both landscape photography (as practiced by, say, Ansel Adams) and railroad photography.

Placing Victor's work in historical context, he was part of an East Coast group of railroad enthusiasts with cameras who traced their inspirational lineages back to the 1920s, '30s, and '40s. These photographers took Lucius Beebe's three-quarter manifesto to heart, accepting it as a template for their own work. Gordon Roth, who befriended Hand in the early 1960s and whom Hand credits as a defining influence, was a staunch proponent of this school, as was Donald Furler, another prominent member of the cadre. Perhaps to a lesser degree, all these men were also affected by the three-quarter work of H. W. Pontin, who prior to Beebe was the Northeast's leading railroad photographer beginning around 1917, with the founding of his Railroad Photographs bureau (later to become Rail Photo Service). The three-quarter approach that both Beebe and Pontin practiced was a codified method that most photographers of the day followed religiously at first; however, as time went on, many, like Hand, began adding their own flourishes to the style.

In Hand's earlier photographs, say from 1958 through 1966, we see an almost reverential devotion to the three-quarter aesthetic. For the most part he's tighter in on the locomotives; he admires their physicality and is adept at emphasizing their power and brawn. Beebe

1. Peter Hales, *William Henry Jackson and the Transformation of the American Landscape* (Philadelphia: Temple University Press, 1989), pp. 213–58.

would have been impressed. But as the 1960s unfold, draw to a close, and the '70s dawn, his vision opens up; deviations soon creep into his frame. New kinds of photos are being made. Hulking locomotives are deemphasized and larger scenic/architectural views get foregrounded more frequently or, at least, share equal status with the railroad. Where Beebe severely truncated the train and its consist from the landscape (as seen in his earlier *Highliners*-era work), Hand now wants to register the train's position within the landscape or cityscape as an integral part of the morphology of its surroundings. This shift in aesthetic intention gets even more dramatic from the 1980s into the 2000s. At this juncture it appears Hand is as much a landscape photographer as a rail enthuiast, for it's apparent that his appreciation for natural wonder and beauty, and the depiction of same, has become as important as capturing the train going by. Hand's pictorial evolution—from tight "three-quarter wedgie" to something more expansive—was informed by three factors: seeing Jackson's nineteenth-century railroad photographs in Lucius Beebe's *Age of Steam* (1957) and *Great Railroad Photographs, U.S.A.* (1964); his extensive foreign travels that began in 1960, giving him access to new, broader vistas that may have left him more awestruck than the landscapes he was accustomed to seeing in America; and his United States Railway Association career in the 1970s, which found him alongside almost every main line on the eastern seaboard, affording him the opportunity to view the railroad landscape and environment with fresh eyes and an evolved kind of scrutiny.

A PHOTO BOOK'S TYPICAL ROLE is to showcase the images printed within its pages, yet it's also important to delve textually into the humanity of the man behind the camera, to give us a fuller understanding of who he is. To that end I want to tell a brief story.

After his good friend David Goodheart suddenly passed away in 2004, Hand took part in a memorial trip (organized by fellow rail enthusiast John Craft) in Goodheart's honor on the Western Maryland Scenic Railroad, a favorite tourist line operation and photographic touchstone for both photographers. The WMSR's lanky 2-8-0 rolled itself and two coaches six miles out to Helmstetter's Curve on an overcast Maryland afternoon with a solemnity befitting the occasion. There, while the many friends of Goodheart remained seated in the coaches, Hand, close buddy Don Phillips, and Goodheart's mother went to the rear vestibule to spread David's ashes on the right-of-way as the train moved slowly along the line. It was a final act of memorialization to celebrate the life of a dear friend and fellow world traveler who shared Hand's love of steam.

Victor would not want it touted, and he will probably urge me to cut those last few lines, but that bigheartedness and fierce loyalty to his friends is a cornerstone of his photography too. There is a resounding "I-gave-it-my-all" passion in his pictures as well as an intrinsic depth to his lifelong pursuit of steam. While some globe-trotting rail enthusiasts of his era shot three or four pictures in a country and then declared they'd "covered it," Hand drilled down and sought a comprehensiveness wherever he went, oftentimes returning to particular countries numerous times. His logbooks, for example, show he spent no fewer than 360 days in South Africa alone (this over the course of three decades) photographing trains. Such layering is the work of a man trying to make the ultimate representation of steam locomotion in a foreign land. This dedication and perseverance are hallmarks of the best work done by other master railroad lensmen, such as Steinheimer, O. Winston Link, Shaughnessy, Philip Hastings, and John Gruber. It is a set of qualities that fosters the creation of visually arresting photographs with staying power.

Ferrocarril Presidente Carlos Antonio López passenger train at Isla Saca, Paraguay, 1991

PERHAPS IT'S A WONDERFUL THING that as we age we begin to see the world as a more expansive place, often more interesting than the confines of our own backyards. Hand was blessed with this state of mind early on; he wasted little time getting overseas in the era before organized tours, routinized global travel, and rental cars made it all so easy and predictable.

The rail enthusiast world has changed in the past twenty years too. Prejudice and provincialism have given way to a more embracing global consciousness; many younger rail enthusiasts now like locomotives regardless of whether they're parked outside a roundhouse in Latvia or one in Louisville. They, like Victor Hand, have made recent treks to the world's far outbacks, encouraged to do so by their ground-breaking predecessors, of which Victor is one.

To say that Hand was a pioneer in tracking down foreign steam is not a false claim. He's more than that. As with any important historical turn in terms of how people do things, it usually takes a supremely confident and fearless individual to move the ball forward. Victor Hand is just such a person. He has provided us with a vision of modern and midcentury steam power in more than fifty countries over the past five decades that is unmatched in scope and quality. Through his photography, drive, ambition, and gumption he has shown us that no place is too far to go when in search of steam.

Plate 1 Western Maryland Scenic Railroad 2-8-0 734 eastbound at Helmstetter's Curve, Maryland, January 19, 2003.

The Western Maryland Scenic Railroad operates tourist trains on the former Western Maryland Railway line between Cumberland and Frostburg, Maryland, using a big 2-8-0 that has been altered to resemble a Western Maryland engine. Railroad photographers found that a group of twenty to thirty people could charter a freight train for a reasonable cost and spend a day along the spectacular line. A number of excellent photographs were possible on the uphill run to Frostburg but, with only fifteen miles of line to work with, the shots became repetitive after a few trips. At my suggestion, engineer Mike Manwiller made a moderate brake application and worked the engine against the brakes going downhill. This worked well and, as this photograph suggests, Manwiller was able to make 734 look as good coming downhill as she did going up.

Figure 1 National Railways of Mexico 4-8-4s are prepared for night freight runs at Valle de Mexico roundhouse north of Mexico City, December 1, 1962.

My father thought that my railroad interest was interfering with my studies. He was right, of course. In 1962 I was going to school in Mexico City to learn Spanish, but my father knew that NdeM was still operating 432 steam locomotives. He visited Mexico City and the usual arguments were made over dinner in his hotel. After dinner, I suggested a visit to the Valle de Mexico roundhouse in the northern suburbs. As we walked around the thirty-four-track roundhouse the air was filled with the smells of steam and oil and the sounds of whistles, turbogenerators, and workmen cursing in Spanish and English. We spent an hour and I took this photograph, which is my favorite. My father never said another word about my obsession.

Figure 2 Norfolk and Western Railway Y-6 2-8-8-2 pushes a coal train up the Blue Ridge grade at Vinton, Virginia, November 1958.

The Norfolk and Western Railway was the last major railroad in the United States to use steam power for large-scale freight operations. I first visited in March of 1958, which was late in the game for steam, but I got to see the N&W many times before the last steam ran in 1960. Located just east of the railroad's headquarters in Roanoke, Virginia, Vinton was a siding where Y-6–class 2-8-8-2s were based to assist heavy coal trains on the steep grades over the Blue Ridge Mountains. With exhaust rising high in the sky, engine 2157 pushes on the rear of an eastbound leaving Vinton. This photograph has a special meaning for me, as it was on this day at Vinton that I met my lifelong friend and traveling companion Don Phillips, who was riding on 2157 up the hill.

Figure 3 Southern Pacific Daylight 4-8-4 eastbound at Macdoel, California, May 16, 1981.

In 1952 my uncle died in California, and my mother took me west for the funeral on a United Airlines DC-6B. One evening we went to Southern Pacific's San Francisco station to see off an aunt who was returning to Los Angeles on the "Lark." I was nine years old but I already liked trains and wanted to see the engine. I still remember finding a big steam locomotive painted orange at the head of the train. It was one of SP's famous Daylight 4-8-4s. Southern Pacific ended steam operations in 1957 and I never expected to see a Daylight run, but in 1975 engine 4449 was pulled from a Portland, Oregon, park and rebuilt. In 1981 Doyle McCormack, who had spearheaded the effort to rebuild 4449, got her repainted in the Daylight colors. I was there for the first trip to Oakland, California, despite being on crutches with a broken leg. The engine has run frequently since, and I have been trackside many times.

Figure 4 Canadian Pacific Royal Hudson 2839 on Southern Railway at Orange, Virginia, March 3, 1979.

CP's streamlined 4-6-4s were called Royal Hudsons because one of them had pulled the Royal Train across Canada in 1939. I saw these engines in their last years pulling commuter trains and freight in Quebec and Ontario. In 1969 three friends and I pooled our money to buy 2839 from Canadian Pacific. Since I was a newly minted lawyer, I was tasked with incorporating a company and negotiating with CP for the purchase and movement of the engine to the United States. My partners had no money for repairs and eventually we all sold our shares. The engine languished in Pennsylvania until 1979, when Southern Railway was looking for a fast engine to power its steam excursions. Southern leased and repaired 2839, and it operated in 1979 and 1980. I found it satisfying to see "my" engine go by at speed.

Plate 2 Mexicano Railway 2-8-0 212 and NdeM 2-8-2 2113 prepare to leave Apizaco, Tlaxcala, with a "Directo" freight train for Mexico City, December 20, 1962.

The Mexican government acquired the Ferrocarril Mexicano in 1946, but it was not merged into the National Railways of Mexico until 1960. Even after the merger, the Mexicano was operated pretty much as a separate railway. Apizaco was the operational hub of the western end of the Mexicano, and it was always a busy place. In this photograph a double-headed Directo, or through freight, is preparing to leave Apizaco in the predawn darkness. The lead engine is an NdeM 2-8-2 dating from the 1920s. The second engine is a Mexicano 2-8-0 built in 1946. These engines were based on the design of the U.S. War Department 2-8-0s, of which more than 2,100 were built for export during and after World War II.

Plate 3 Nevada Northern Railway 4-6-0 40 with a mixed train at Hiline, Nevada, November 1, 1992.

The Nevada Northern Railway was built in 1906 to serve the Kennecott Copper Corporation facilities around Ely, Nevada. When the Kennecott smelter at McGill closed in 1983, the railroad was closed. After the shutdown Kennecott doanated much of its equipment and facilities to the White Pine Historical Railroad Foundation, which has preserved the railroad facilities in the Ely area as an operating railroad museum. The complex is recognized as one of the most complete examples of a steam-era yard and shop facility remaining in North America. Locomotive 40 was built for the Nevada Northern by Baldwin Locomotive Works in 1910. It was rebuilt by volunteers at the museum and in recent years has often pulled excursion trains of vintage equipment.

Plate 4 Double-headed Soviet Railways SO-17-class 2-10-0s at Malinitci, Ukraine, February 22, 1994.

When steam locomotive production ended in 1957 there were about 36,000 steam locomotives on Soviet Railways. The Soviet Union had a centrally planned economy and everything on the railways was standardized, including locomotives. When a successful engine was designed, it was reproduced in large numbers, in many cases for decades. More than 5,000 SO-class 2-10-0s were produced between 1935 and 1954. This photograph shows two of the later examples of the class pulling a freight train in southwestern Ukraine. One locomotive burns coal, the other oil.

Plate 5 Soo Line 4-6-2 with a passenger train crossing the St. Croix River at Cedar Bend, near Osceola, Wisconsin, August 3, 1998.

The Soo Line Railroad last operated steam locomotives in regular service in 1955, but a number of locomotives remained operational for several years and were used on annual excursion trains. The last such trip operated between Minneapolis, Minnesota, and Ladysmith, Wisconsin, with 4-6-2 2719 in June of 1959. I knew about this trip but was unable to get out to the Midwest at that time to ride it. I often thought about the missed opportunity to see one of Soo Line's attractive engines, and I had my chance thirty-eight years later, when 2719 was rebuilt for use at the Lake Superior Railroad Museum in Duluth, Minnesota.

Plate 6 British Railways Britannia 4-6-2 at the engine terminal in Rugby, England, September 3, 1963.

After nationalization of the railways in 1948, British Railways designed and built a series of twelve standard types of locomotives to supplement the engines that had been inherited from the predecessor railways. These engines were designed to be simple, efficient, and easy to maintain. The Britannia-class 4-6-2 was the design settled on for a large "mixed traffic" engine that would be capable of handling freight traffic as well as express passenger workings. The first Britannia appeared in 1951, and fifty-five had been built by 1955. They were quite successful and eventually worked all over Britain.

Plate 7 Canadian Pacific Railway 4-6-4 2816 westbound at Massive, Alberta, May 1, 2006.

In the late 1950s I often visited Quebec to photograph the last steam operations on the Canadian Pacific Railway. Hudson 2816 was one of several dozen modern CPR locomotives that operated in passenger service out of Montreal until May 1960. I photographed it on several occasions, and the handsome locomotive was one of my favorites. The engine was a museum piece for the next thirty-five years until CPR leased it and had the engine rebuilt. The locomotive made its debut in 2001 as Canadian Pacific's "corporate ambassador," and it has run all over CP's system. It looked particularly good pulling a Calgary–Lake Louise special train along the Bow River in the Canadian Rockies.

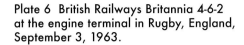

Plate 8 British Railways goods train bound for Perth at Forteviot, Scotland, January 31, 1964.

The Scottish countryside provides plenty of pleasant backdrops for railway photography. When the weather was bad I usually just watched the trains. Once in a while a scene presented itself that made an interesting photograph despite the dull weather. In this photograph, a northbound goods train behind a Black Five 4-6-0 runs through Strathearn (the valley of the river Earn) on its way from Carstairs to Perth. The calm river and the rugged Ochil Hills behind the train create a lovely scene. Sheep may safely graze.

Plate 9 National Railways of Mexico 4-8-4 3045 works upgrade through a thunderstorm at Bernal, Querétaro, June 15, 1964.

The National Railways of Mexico operated two trunk lines north of Mexico City that roughly paralleled each other. Freight trains ran on a directional basis on these lines. Most through freight trains were powered by NdeM's thirty-two compact 4-8-4s. In the spring of 1964 I was in the area when a wreck closed the southbound line, causing a back-log of seven trains to build up at San Nicolás at the foot of the mountain grade to Escandón. My fellow photographers and I found a location on the grade, and when the wreck was cleared the seven trains came up the hill. By the time the last train reached us a thunderstorm had moved in, and I got soaked taking this photograph. Two days later I had a fever of 104° and had to retreat to a hotel in Mexico City, where the hotel doctor diagnosed pneumonia, gave me penicillin, and suggested a few days' rest.

Plate 10 French National Railways Pacific 231.G 285 from atop the coaling tower at Le Mans, France, August 20, 1964.

I visited Le Mans in 1964 with my friends Ronald Wright and Howard Fine. One morning we visited the engine terminal and decided to climb the ladders to the roof of the concrete coaling tower. From the top, two semicircular roundhouses and two turntables could be seen, along with ash pits and water columns for servicing the engines assigned to Le Mans. More than one hundred locomotives were in view, and activity was constant as engines went through the fire cleaning, coaling, and lubrication processes. Several hours later, I was getting hungry, but no one wanted to leave. I climbed down the ladder, drove to a nearby shop, and brought back bread and cheese for a picnic among the cinders on the coaling tower roof.

Plate 11 Management and train crew confer on the station platform at Le Havre, France, September 7, 1964.

French National Railways express train 103 left Gare St-Lazare in Paris at 8:45 a.m., and was eight minutes late arriving at Le Havre. As passengers stream off the train, the superintendent is on the platform wanting to know why the train was delayed. Each participant in the conversation can be identified by his uniform—the superintendent in his business suit and hat, the station master wearing a white hat, the car inspector in overalls, and the grimy engineer, or *mécanicien*, trying to explain what delayed him. The fireman in the engine cab eyes the photographer with an amused look while he enjoys his cigarette. He is staying out of the argument. The locomotive is 231.D 767, built for the Chemin de Fer de L'État after the First World War and modernized by the French National Railways.

Plate 12 South African Railways 19D-class 4-8-2 2692 approaches the Lootsberg Pass at Blouwater, Cape Province, June 4, 1992.

Winter on the Lootsberg Pass can produce some cold weather. South African Railways' Mosselbaai main line crosses the Sneeuberg Mountains in the eastern part of Cape Province. The steepest part of the climb is between Blouwater, at the southern end of the Lootsberg Pass, and the summit at Lootsberg siding. In this seven-mile section the railway climbs 800 feet. The country is desolate, with only a few sheep farms, and in winter sometimes sees heavy snowfall. The locomotive in this photograph is a 19D-class 4-8-2 built in 1938, which has been equipped with a long tender to extend its range between water stops.

Plate 13 Interior view of Eastleigh Locomotive Works on British Railways' Southern Region, September 3, 1964.

In 1964 I spent six weeks in Europe with my good friends Ronald Wright and Howard Fine. We were in Bournemouth, England, photographing Southern Region Pacifics when Fine read in a British rail magazine that Eastleigh Works was open to the public on Saturday afternoons. Eastleigh was the major locomotive shop of the Southern Region of British Railways, and it was only thirty-five miles from where we were staying. We presented ourselves shortly after noon and were given the run of the shop. In this photograph, the boiler and frame of West Country–class 4-6-2 34019 "Bideford" are being refurbished. The wheels and machinery are in other parts of the shop for work. We spent an interesting few hours, then went on our way.

Plate 14 Japanese National Railways 4-6-4 C62-24 starts a local passenger train north out of Taira, Honshū, June 22, 1966.

Growing up in New York City, I often visited the New York Central Railroad station at Harmon, New York, where trains from Grand Central Terminal exchanged their electric locomotives for steam or diesel locomotives for the run west. Heavy traffic made Harmon an exciting place, and I found other such places in my worldwide travels. Le Mans, France, was one, where trains from Paris to points in Brittany and western France changed locomotives. Miranda de Ebro was another, on the Spanish National Railways line from the French border to Madrid. In Japan, the place to be was Taira. In the mid-1960s, Taira was as far north as electrification extended on the Jōban Line, and heavy passenger traffic from Tōkyō's Ueno Station to the cities of northern Honshū exchanged electric locomotives for the biggest and best of Japan's steamers.

Plate 15 Inspection pits at South African Railways' Beaconsfield locomotive shed in Kimberley, Cape Province, August 31, 1965.

South African Railways had a fleet of more than 1,300 modern, high-powered steam locomotives built between 1935 and 1958. In the 1960s these big engines monopolized service on the main lines, but many smaller engines survived to serve on branch lines with light rail or for yard shunting. In this photograph, a low-drivered class 8A 4-8-0 dating from 1902 shares space on the inspection pits at the huge locomotive facility in Kimberley with one of its larger cousins, built more than fifty years later.

Plate 16 Union Pacific Railroad 4-8-4 8444 lays over at Oakley, Kansas, August 27, 1986.

Union Pacific 4-8-4 844 (renumbered 8444) was never retired by the railroad. It was one of the last steam locomotives in regular service and has enjoyed a more than fifty-year career pulling special trains all over the UP system. Steam excursions rarely ran on the Kansas City–Denver route but, in the summer of 1986, 8444 ventured onto the lightly trafficked line. The engine spent the night amid the grain elevators at Oakley, Kansas, and since the location had little ambient light it presented a good opportunity for night flash photography. There wasn't much to do in Oakley that night, and after a few shots I went to bed early.

Plate 17 Two mixed trains meet on the Devil's Nose switchbacks on the Guayaquil and Quito Railway near Sibambe, Ecuador, July 11, 1996.

The mountain section of the Guayaquil and Quito Railway between Bucay and Palmira Pass climbs 9,651 feet in forty-nine miles. The most spectacular part of the climb is up Nariz del Diablo, or the Devil's Nose, a 1,000-foot-high mountain at the junction of the Chanchan and Alausi rivers. The railway climbs the Devil's Nose by means of switchbacks or zigzag tracks cut into the mountainside. The steepest part of the hill is on a 5.5 percent gradient. In this photograph two trains are seen after meeting at the upper zigzag. The lower train is backing downgrade to the lower zigzag, hidden in the Alausi canyon to the left. From there it will reverse direction and continue into the Sibambe station at the base of the mountain. The upper train is accelerating uphill away from the upper zigzag on its way to Alausi.

Plate 18 Guayaquil and Quito Railway 2-8-0 53 climbs the upper level of the switchbacks on the Devil's Nose near Sibambe, Ecuador, August 17, 2003.

The Guayaquil and Quito Railway was surveyed and built between 1898 and 1908 by an American company headed by Archer Harman. It is one of the most impressive examples of railway engineering in the world. It was built through thick jungle and rough mountain territory and under severe climatic conditions. Surveyors and construction workers traveled by mule train and all earth moving was done by hand. Equipment, track, and bridge material were all imported from the United States. In this photograph a short freight train climbs a steep grade high above the Alausi River. The train has just traversed the two switchbacks cut into the side of the mountain known as the Devil's Nose.

Plate 19 Pennsylvania Railroad 4-4-2 7002 and 4-4-0 1223 crossing the Susquehanna River at Rockville, Pennsylvania, June 8, 1985.

After the Pennsylvania Railroad ended steam operations in 1957, the management set aside examples of many types of the railroad's distinctive steam locomotives. These engines eventually became part of the collection of the Railroad Museum of Pennsylvania at Strasburg. Several of the smaller engines were leased by the Strasburg Railroad, a short line that rebuilt the engines and operated them on tourist trains. These engines rarely left Strasburg, but on one memorable weekend in 1985, 4-4-0 1223 and 4-4-2 7002 teamed up to haul a circle trip from Strasburg to Harrisburg over former Pennsylvania Railroad lines. The train crossed the Susquehanna River on the famous Rockville Bridge, built in 1901–2. The four-track bridge is the longest and widest stone arch bridge in the world.

Plate 20 Atchison, Topeka and Santa Fe Railway 4-8-4 3751 on the Grand Canyon Railway at Willaha, Arizona, August 23, 2002.

In May 1960 I was riding on Missouri Pacific Railroad's "Missouri River Eagle," en route from St. Louis to Omaha. Approaching Kansas City I saw a long line of retired Santa Fe Railway steam locomotives outside the Sheffield Steel mill. I got off the train at Kansas City and found my way back to the mill. I walked the line of twenty-one 4-8-4s and twenty 2-10-4s, knowing they would soon be turned into rebar. I never forgot how huge those engines were. I got my first chance to see a Santa Fe 4-8-4 in action in 1992, when 3751 was returned to service by the San Bernardino Railroad Historical Society. The 1927 Baldwin engine had been on display in San Bernardino, California, since its retirement in the 1950s.

Plate 21 Mexicano Railway 2-8-0 210 in the roundhouse at Apizaco, Tlaxcala, September 1, 1962.

The Ferrocarril Mexicano was the first trunk line railway built in Mexico. The line was purchased by the Mexican government in 1946 but continued to operate as a separate railway until 1960. The Mexicano had a distinctive roster of locomotives, including 2-8-0 210, one of a group of eleven engines built for the railway by Baldwin in 1921. In the early 1960s these locomotives were regular performers on the twice-daily mixed trains between Puebla and the main line at Apizaco.

Plate 22 British Railways 5015 "Kingswear Castle" at speed on the Western Region main line, December 26, 1961.

I first went to Britain in the winter of 1961. I had seen pictures of British Railways engines and was especially impressed by the former Great Western Railway locomotives operating on the Western Region. First stop in London was Paddington Station, where I found plenty of activity. I rode a train to Reading, stayed an hour, and continued on to Swindon. Somewhere on the Western Region main line, the train I was riding began to overtake a train on a parallel track going slightly slower. I opened the window and leaned out to take this photograph of a Castle pulling the 11:55 a.m. ex–Paddington–Milford Haven express.

Plate 23 Two Chinese QJ 2-10-2s power an eastbound freight train on the Ji-Tong Railway at Tunnel 4 near Da Ying Zi, January 15, 2004.

The Ji-Tong Railway was built 585 miles across Inner Mongolia to provide a direct route between China's industrial northeast and the western part of the country. The railway was completed in 1995 and bypassed Beijing and other major cities. For cost reasons it was initially powered with secondhand QJ 2-10-2s acquired from China Rail. High point of the line was the 4,175-foot summit of the Jingpeng Pass. The railway was engineered to high standards, with huge concrete viaducts and several tunnels, and was the last in the world to operate a heavy mainline freight service with steam locomotives. The big show ended in 2005.

Plate 24 Spanish National Railways 2-8-0 takes water at the locomotive depot at Valladolid, January 24, 1965.

Red Nacional de los Ferrocarriles Españoles (RENFE), the Spanish National Railways, presented the photographer with an endless variety of subject matter in the 1960s. Modern steam locomotives and fast Talgo diesel trains could be photographed alongside engines fifty or a hundred years old. Valladolid was a major terminal on the Northern Railway, which became part of RENFE in 1941. The engine terminal was always busy. RENFE finally ended steam locomotive operations in 1975.

Plate 25 A laborer cleans the fire on South African Railways GD 2-6-2+2-6-2 Garratt 2231 at Alicedale, Cape Province, August 24, 1965.

Steam locomotives were labor-intensive machines. Probably the toughest and dirtiest job involved in servicing a coal-burning steam locomotive was cleaning the fire. Long metal rakes were used to scrape hot clinker and ash from the fire grate into the ash pan, which was then emptied into a pit under the tracks. It was a nasty job. Thirteen GD engines were built by Beyer-Peacock in 1925–26. They spent most of their working lives hauling trains on the steeply graded branch between Alicedale and Port Alfred, in the eastern part of Cape Province. The GDs were retired in 1968, three years after this picture was taken.

Plate 26 Japanese National Railways C-61-class 4-6-4 starts a passenger train out of Ikarigaseki, Honshū, in a blizzard, January 21, 1971.

In 1966 I planned a visit to Japan. A friend introduced me to the late Ed Delvers, an American rail enthusiast living in Tōkyō. Delvers knew the publisher of *Japan Railfan* magazine, and Kentaro Hirai and Kenichi Matsumoto, who published railway books. On arrival, I met with these people and was advised of where to go to see JNR's remaining big steam locomotives. I kept in touch with the publishers for a number of years, and sent them many photographs that were printed in Japanese publications. One of the suggestions made by my Japanese friends was to visit Ikarigaseki, a scenic location in far northern Honshū. On the day I visited, the scenery was obscured by a blizzard but the photographs turned out fine.

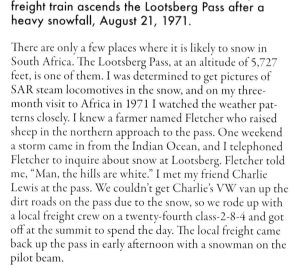

Plate 27 Northbound South African Railways freight train ascends the Lootsberg Pass after a heavy snowfall, August 21, 1971.

There are only a few places where it is likely to snow in South Africa. The Lootsberg Pass, at an altitude of 5,727 feet, is one of them. I was determined to get pictures of SAR steam locomotives in the snow, and on my three-month visit to Africa in 1971 I watched the weather patterns closely. I knew a farmer named Fletcher who raised sheep in the northern approach to the pass. One weekend a storm came in from the Indian Ocean, and I telephoned Fletcher to inquire about snow at Lootsberg. Fletcher told me, "Man, the hills are white." I met my friend Charlie Lewis at the pass. We couldn't get Charlie's VW van up the dirt roads on the pass due to the snow, so we rode up with a local freight crew on a twenty-fourth class-2-8-4 and got off at the summit to spend the day. The local freight came back up the pass in early afternoon with a snowman on the pilot beam.

Plate 28 Three ex–Chicago and North Western 2-8-0s are readied for night runs on National Railways of Mexico at Tierra Blanca, Veracruz, October 20, 1962.

After World War II, National Railways of Mexico invested substantial sums of money to modernize its facilities, but the modernization program did not reach the more remote areas of the country. In the early 1960s the lines from Veracruz to the Isthmus of Tehuantepec and on to the Guatemalan border were still steam powered and facilities were fairly primitive. The engine shed at Tierra Blanca was a ramshackle building made of old rail and corrugated steel siding, but it kept the rain off the mechanics' heads.

Plate 29 New Zealand Government Railways class J 4-8-2 1237 at the station in Greymouth, South Island, June 13, 1967.

Winter on New Zealand's South Island is often snowy, but on the Tasman Sea coast at Greymouth I had to do my night photography in a steady drizzle. Keeping my Speed Graphic dry involved using a homemade contraption made of plastic bags, with a flap in back to allow film holders to be inserted and the dark slide to be removed as required. The lens was of course covered until the last minute, and once it was exposed to the rain the flashbulbs had to be fired quickly to avoid raindrops or mist on the lens. The rain did add to the allure of night photographs, with the wet rails and wet locomotive reflecting light and white steam condensing in the cold drizzle.

Plate 30 Freight train passing Denver and Rio Grande Western water tank at Cresco, Colorado, October 3, 1967.

During the 1870s and '80s more than two thousand miles of narrow-gauge railroads were built in the Rocky Mountains to tap the mineral wealth of the area. As the mines played out these lines were abandoned, and by 1956 the three-foot-gauge system operated by the Denver and Rio Grande Western Railroad was only 293 miles in length. From a standard-gauge connection at Alamosa, Colorado, the line crossed Cumbres Pass at an elevation of 10,015 feet and descended to Chama, New Mexico. From there the line ran west to Durango, Colorado, with branches to Farmington, New Mexico, and Silverton, Colorado. The freight operation was a remnant of another era. It was a narrow-gauge mountain railroad operated with a fleet of steam locomotives built in the 1920s, and many of the freight cars dated from the first decade of the century. The Rio Grande was expecting to abandon the line and nothing was modernized.

Plate 31 Western Maryland Scenic Railroad 2-8-0 734 entering Brush Tunnel on the former Western Maryland Railway Connellsville line in Maryland, January 18, 2003.

Standing inside a tunnel while a train passes is usually a dangerous thing to do, as clearances can be tight and something might be hanging off the train that could cause injury. Brush Tunnel on the Western Maryland Scenic Railroad was an exception, since the Western Maryland Railway Connellsville Extension had been built as a double track railroad. With one track removed, there was plenty of room for a photographer to stand safely. I ventured into the tunnel to photograph 2-8-0 734 hauling a chartered freight train upgrade. The noise the engine exhaust made in the tunnel was earsplitting, and the bore filled with smoke and steam. What a fine show to watch and photograph!

Plate 32 British Railways A-1-class Pacific 60147 "North Eastern" at Edinburgh, Scotland, January 1, 1962.

The A-1 Pacifics were designed by A. H. Peppercorn, who was the chief mechanical engineer of the London & North Eastern Railway from 1946 until it became part of British Railways in 1948. Forty-nine of these handsome three-cylinder locomotives were built in 1948 and 1949. They joined the fleet of more than two hundred 4-6-2s that were the backbone of express passenger motive power on the East Coast main line of the former LNER. By the time I got to England some of the primary duties of the Pacifics on the East Coast main line had been taken over by diesels, but there were still plenty of steam locomotives running.

Plate 33 British Railways locomotives on the ready tracks at York, England, August 29, 1963.

York was a major railway center on the East Coast main line, which ran between London and Edinburgh, Scotland. I first photographed at York in 1961 and 1962, when the East Coast main line was mostly steam operated. The line was part of the London & North Eastern Railway prior to the 1948 formation of British Railways and had always been a raceway for LNER's large fleet of 4-6-2 locomotives. By the time I returned to York, in 1963, the East Coast main line was in the process of being dieselized, although there was still plenty of steam around. In this photograph, two 4-6-2s, two 2-6-2s, and two 4-6-0s share the ready track with three new diesel locomotives.

Plate 34 Turkish State Railways 2-10-0 56724 with a westbound freight train at Gumus, September 15, 1973.

Turkish State Railways still operated a major part of its system with steam locomotives when I visited in the early 1970s. The locomotives were big, some of the scenery was spectacular, the people were friendly, and food and travel conditions were pretty good. The main line from eastern Turkey and Adana to Istanbul and Ankara ran through the Taurus Mountains and provided excellent and plentiful photographic opportunities.

Plate 35 Anshan Iron and Steel Company blast furnaces are serviced by an SY 2-8-2, Anshan, China, January 15, 1995.

I traveled to northern China in January 1995 with my longtime friend Greg Triplett, a well-known Australian railway photographer. Triplett planned the trip, and the main goal was to obtain winter action photographs of heavy freight trains. Several industrial railway operations were also included in the itinerary. At Anshan we visited a large integrated steel mill operated by the Anshan Iron and Steel Company. The technology of the mill was pure 1930s, with towering blast furnaces, coke ovens, open slag dumps, and mill locomotives moving cars of molten iron amid the steam and smoke. It was a fascinating view of old-fashioned heavy industry.

Plate 36 Grand Trunk Western Railroad 4-8-4 6319 at Pontiac, Michigan, after hauling a commuter train from Detroit, December 21, 1959.

Grand Trunk Western was a subsidiary of Canadian National Railways that operated CN's lines in Michigan, Indiana, and Illinois. The railroad operated its fleet of modern steam locomotives into the late 1950s. By 1959 steam operation was concentrated in the Detroit area, and the last regularly scheduled steam-operated passenger trains in the United States were a set of four commuter trains running out of Detroit. Northern 6319 rests near the coal dock in Pontiac after bringing train 77 from Detroit. Three months later the service was dieselized, ending steam passenger operation in the United States.

Plate 37 Mississippian Railway 2-8-0 77 with a freight train at Smithville, Mississippi, October 4, 1986.

The Mississippian Railway was a short line that ran twenty-four miles from Amory to Fulton, Mississippi. It connected with the St. Louis–San Francisco Railway at Amory. The line continued to use its two ex-SLSF 2-8-0s in regular freight service until 1966. After the railroad was dieselized, number 77 remained on the property and saw occasional use when diesel locomotives were not available. In 1985 the engine was restored for use on passenger excursions.

Plate 38 Irún–Madrid express on the Spanish National Railways at Pancorbo, Spain, January 27, 1965.

The most heavily graded portions of RENFE's Madrid–Irún main line had been electrified by the 1960s, but between Ávila and Miranda de Ebro the line was steam operated except for a few Talgo express trains. I was drawn to this line to see the ten Confederation 4-8-4s, the ultimate development of Spanish steam locomotives. Introduced in 1956, these massive engines were very impressive taking charge of express passenger trains at Miranda de Ebro. Here we see a 4-8-4 assisted by a modern RENFE 141F 2-8-2, climbing the grade out of the Ebro River valley with train 10, the southbound "Iberia Express." The weather was grim but the railway action was wonderful.

Plate 39 15E-class 4-8-2s rest at South African Railways Bethlehem locomotive shed in the Orange Free State, August 18, 1965.

SAR operated coal-burning steam locomotives much later than most railways in the world, and for a number of reasons. Coal was available, labor was cheap, and the railway had a large stock of more than 1,300 modern steam locomotives built between 1935 and 1958. The main reason steam lasted so long in South Africa, however, had to do with politics. In 1948 the Nationalist Party took power and began to implement a policy of apartheid, or separation of the races. South Africa became an international pariah, and economic sanctions were imposed by many countries. One of the effects of the sanctions was to limit oil imports. Eventually, labor costs and the economics of diesel locomotives caught up with South African Railways, and steam locomotives began to be retired in large numbers. When the political situation changed in the 1990s the remaining steam operations ended.

Plate 40 Norfolk and Western Railway class A westbound at Bluefield, West Virginia, August 4, 1987.

Norfolk and Western Railway built 43 class A 2-6-6-4 articulated locomotives between 1936 and 1950 for fast freight service. These superb engines served the railroad until the end of regular steam operations in 1960. Engine 1218 was displayed at the Roanoke Transportation Museum and was eventually reacquired by Norfolk and Western. When a second big engine was needed for service on Norfolk Southern's extensive steam excursion program, the big articulated was sent to the NS steam shop in Birmingham, Alabama, to be rebuilt. The 1218 made its debut in excursion service in April 1987 and was a star attraction at the 1987 convention of the National Railway Historical Society in Roanoke. Several days later 1218 hauled a hopper train from Roanoke, Virginia, to Bluefield, West Virginia, to position the engine for a passenger excursion to Kenova, West Virginia. It is seen here entering Bluefield past trainloads of coal that are earning the money to pay for its operation.

Plate 41 Two South African Railways GEA-class 4-8-2+2-8-4 Garratts are under the coal dock at Greyville locomotive shed in Durban, Natal, August 10, 1965.

At major locomotive terminals South African Railways erected high-capacity steel coaling stations. A ramp allowed gondolas of coal to be shoved to the top of the bunker, where the coal was unloaded by gravity, or if it was in older gondolas by men with shovels. If you were lucky enough to be around when cars were being pushed up the steep ramp it was quite a show. The ramps were of light construction, so smaller and older engines performed this duty, and they usually got a pretty good run before they hit the ramp with two or three cars of coal.

Plate 42 British Railways 7026 "Tenby Castle" leaving Wolverhampton, England, June 14, 1962.

It was the lure of the Great Western Railway that first attracted me to Britain. I had read of the great engineering works of I. K. Brunel and had seen photographs of the Great Western's attractive locomotives. This photograph embodies all that was great about the GWR—distinctive locomotives, signals, tunnels, and bridges. The Castle-class 4-6-0s were first introduced in 1923 and became the standard GWR express passenger locomotive. They were built through 1950, and the class eventually numbered 181 locomotives. The Great Western made extensive use of lower quadrant semaphore signals. The brick tunnel portal and flyover bridge above were typical of the high standards to which everything on GWR was built. The train is "The Cornishman," the 9:55 a.m. express from Wolverhampton to Penzance.

Plate 43 Spanish National Railways roundhouse at Soria, January 30, 1965.

This book contains quite a few examples of night flash photography. Some of the photographs involve the use of synchronized flashbulbs to photograph moving trains, while others are made by "painting with light." This involves lighting a stationary train with a number of flashbulbs in sequence, which allows the photographer to carefully control the lighting. Every once in a while a night scene presents itself that needs no additional light. In this photograph the dim incandescent bulbs in the Soria roundhouse illuminate the steam-filled interior of the building. I considered providing this composition with fill-in light on the front of the locomotives but decided it was better without flashbulbs.

Plate 44 Union Pacific Railroad 4-6-6-4 3985 lays a thick trail of smoke across the plains at Wyoming, Wyoming, June 16, 1982.

In the summer of 1959 my friend Don Phillips and I were riding on an excursion train out of St. Paul when we heard from other rail enthusiasts that two major railroads were using steam locomotives during a sudden upswing in freight traffic. Canadian National was running steam out of Winnipeg, Manitoba, and Union Pacific was operating several dozen engines out of Cheyenne, Wyoming. The lure of Union Pacific's "Big Boy" 4-8-8-4s and "Challenger" 4-6-6-4s was too great, and that night we headed to Cheyenne. Unfortunately, we were a month too late. A steel strike had reduced traffic levels and the steamers were all dead in the huge Cheyenne roundhouse awaiting a call back to duty that never came. I got my chance to see a UP Challenger in operation twenty-three years later when the railroad returned locomotive 3985 to service.

Plate 45 Four French National Railways 2-8-2s in the locomotive depot at Le Mans, July 7, 1963.

In the early 1960s Le Mans was the end of electrification of SNCF's Western Region main line out of Gare Montparnasse in Paris. From Le Mans, main lines radiated to major cities in Brittany and the lower Loire Valley. On the outskirts of the city was a large freight marshaling yard and a locomotive terminal to service the hundreds of steam locomotives operating west of Le Mans. A large allocation of 141.P-class 2-8-2s were the mainstay of the motive power on freight and secondary passenger trains. The 141.Ps were an advanced design from the famous locomotive designer André Chapelon. They were four-cylinder compound locomotives equipped with stokers and other modern appliances; 318 of these engines were built from 1942 to 1952. They remained in service until the late 1960s.

Plate 46 Buffalo Creek & Gauley Railroad hopper train at Avoca, West Virginia, June 5, 1963.

After the major railroads ended steam operations in the United States, a few short line railroads continued to haul freight trains with steam power. The last surviving West Virginia short line to do so was the Buffalo Creek & Gauley Railroad, which operated an eighteen-mile line between Dundon and Widen, West Virginia, with four 2-8-0s. The reason for the railroad's existence was a coal mine at Widen. The line interchanged traffic with the Baltimore & Ohio's Grafton to Charleston line at Dundon. When the mine shut down in 1963 so did the railroad.

Plate 47 Maclear branch passenger train eastbound on South African Railways at Glen Wallace, Cape Province, August 6, 1971.

The Maclear branch ran 173 miles in the foothills of the Stormberg range and featured some beautiful scenery. Standard locomotives on the line were 19D-class 4-8-2s. The line had a daylight passenger train and several freights in each direction, and fairly good roads made following trains easy for a photographer. In this photograph, 19D 2665, built by Krupp in 1939, pulls the 7:45 a.m. ex–Maclear-Sterkstroom passenger train on its last lap into Sterkstroom. I spent several days on this line during an extended visit to South Africa in 1971 and found the photography rewarding.

Plate 48 British Railways engine driver on the foot plate of Britannia Pacific 70041 "Sir John Moore," running on the former Great Central Railway main line, August 27, 1963.

It was difficult to get a ride on a locomotive in Great Britain. I once approached the driver of a Princess Royal 4-6-2 about to leave Carlisle with an express for Glasgow and asked for a cab ride. I was told in no uncertain terms, in a thick Scottish brogue, that "It is a criminal offense to allow unauthorized persons on the foot plate." There are exceptions to every rule. I met a fellow photographer at Leicester who had a good friend who was the regular driver of a fish train that ran between Grimsby and Bristol. This driver's run was from Lincoln to Leicester on the former Great Central Railway via Clipstone Junction and Nottingham. He invited me to ride with him. The train came in to Lincoln with a Britannia 4-6-2 on the head end, and the new crew took over. What a ride it was!

Plate 49 Drive wheels and rods of Union Pacific Railroad 4-8-4 8444 at Cheyenne, Wyoming, May 9, 1968.

Union Pacific 4-8-4 844 was built in 1944 by American Locomotive Company, the last steam locomotive built for UP. Steam operations continued on Union Pacific on a seasonal basis into the summer of 1959. I visited Cheyenne just after the railroad terminated steam use, and I was heartbroken that I had missed the big show. When I heard that an excursion train would run from Cheyenne to Rawlins, Wyoming, in the fall of 1960 I made a point to be there to photograph the 844 in action. In 1962 the engine was renumbered 8444 to make way for a new diesel locomotive, but the 4-8-4 outlived the diesel and regained its old number in 1989. The 844 was a favorite of mine and I went west quite often to see it.

Plate 50 Ferrocarriles Argentinos double-headed mixed train near Lepá, October 12, 1991.

Argentine Railways' Esquel branch was a 250-mile narrow-gauge line operated as a branch of the broad-gauge Ferrocarril General Roca. It diverged from the San Carlos de Bariloche line at Ingeniero Jacobacci and ran south to the resort town of Esquel through barren and unpopulated country. The line was operated with a fleet of thirty-seven small 2-8-2s built by Baldwin in the United States and Henschel in Germany in 1922 for proposed lines in Patagonia that were never built. When the Esquel line was being built in the 1940s these engines were assembled and put into service. Fifty years later they were still at work in the dry and barren landscape of the Andes foothills.

Plate 51 Helper locomotive on Denver and Rio Grande Western pipe train at Los Pinos, Colorado, October 9, 1967.

In the early 1950s natural gas was discovered in northwestern New Mexico. Large quantities of steel pipe were required to extract and transport the gas. The highways in the mountainous area were poorly developed, and the task of transporting this freight fell to the only railroad in the area, the Denver and Rio Grande Western's narrow-gauge line. In the 1950s and early '60s the line boomed but the operation was conducted much as it had been earlier in the century. Motive power was supplied by a group of 2-8-2s built in the 1920s, and dispatching was done by old-fashioned telegraph and train order. Mikado 483, built by Baldwin in 1925, is seen here acting as a mid-train helper engine, pushing hard on loads of pipe to get the train around the horseshoe curve at Los Pinos.

Plate 52 Denver and Rio Grande Western Railroad freight train, Los Pinos, Colorado, October 9, 1967.

The pipe traffic moving from Pueblo, Colorado, to Farmington, New Mexico, to supply the northern New Mexico gas fields extended the life of the Rio Grande narrow-gauge freight operation for a number of years, but by the mid-1960s the pipe movements were beginning to decline. There was scant other freight on the line. All freight had to be transloaded between standard-gauge and narrow-gauge equipment at Alamosa, which of course added to the expense of the operation. By the mid-1960s operations were down to one set of trains per week, and abandonment was inevitable. In this photograph 2-8-2 487 is rounding the curve approaching the water tank at Los Pinos, with engine 483 cut in mid-train as a helper.

Plate 53 China Rail freight trains meet at dusk at Sha Pi Tou siding, January 12, 1993.

The QJ-class 2-10-2 was the standard steam freight locomotive in China in the last three decades of steam operation. The name Qian Jin means "march forward." An estimated 4,700 of these locomotives were built in China between 1959 and 1988. The design was based on a Russian 2-10-2, which in turn had been based on American locomotives supplied to the Soviet Union before World War II. Given China's abundant coal reserves and cheap labor, it is not surprising that some of these engines operated until 2005 and were the last steam locomotives used in heavy freight service in the world.

Plate 54 Nickel Plate Road 2-8-4 759 at the Erie-Lackawanna Railroad terminal at Hoboken, New Jersey, October 10, 1969.

Nickel Plate Road 759 was the first large steam locomotive in the United States to be restored by a private owner, and it ran on many trips between 1968 and 1973. Ross E. Rowland, a New York commodities trader, owned the engine and financed its operation. Rowland liked big steam engines and was involved in rebuilding and operating a number of locomotives over a thirty-year period. He often was at the throttle on these trips. It was a thrill to see a big engine go by at high speed, with the throttle wide open and Rowland leaning out of the cab.

Plate 55 Milwaukee Road 4-8-4 261 in the fog at Gouldsboro, Pennsylvania, February 20, 1996.

The Chicago, Milwaukee, St. Paul and Pacific Railroad took delivery of ten class S-3 4-8-4s from American Locomotive Company in 1944. The S-3s had short service lives, and after retirement in 1954 the 261 was donated to the National Railroad Museum in Green Bay, Wisconsin. In 1992 the engine was leased by North Star Rail, and under the direction of Steve Sandberg and his father, Frank, the group rebuilt the locomotive. It first ran on excursion trains in 1993 and has been active since. In 1995 the group took the engine to Scranton, Pennsylvania, to participate in the opening celebrations for the Steamtown National Historic Site, and it remained in the east for almost a year.

Plate 56 China Rail westbound freight leaves a deep cut on the grade at Meng Jia Wan, January 13, 1993.

The main line that connects Beijing with Lanzhou and northwestern China follows the upper part of the Yellow River valley for hundreds of miles. On the section between Zhongwei and Gantang the line climbs a stiff grade out of the river valley. In the 1990s pairs of QJ 2-10-0s handled the frequent trains in all weather. Every twenty minutes or so an uphill train went by with two QJs (sometimes three) working hard, and the downhill trains drifted quietly by.

Plate 57 Belgrano Railway 2-10-2 1354 crosses the Viaducto Polvorillo west of San Antonio de los Cobres, Argentina, September 26, 1972.

I first visited Argentina in 1971. I had read about the Antofagasta-Salta Railway, a spectacular line through the Andes linking Argentina and Chile. Begun in 1929 the line was not completed until 1948. Built to meter gauge, the Salta-Socompa section was operated as a part of Argentine Railways Ferrocarril General Belgrano. Between Salta and San Antonio de los Cobres the line climbed 8,540 feet in 122 miles. At one point you could look off a ridge and see seven levels of track below. On my first trip I was by myself and on short time, but I knew I had to return to photograph this railway properly. I did so in 1972 in company with my friends Harold Edmonson and Charlie Lewis.

Plate 58 Duluth, Missabe & Iron Range Railway 2-8-8-4 under the coal dock at Proctor, Minnesota, July 3, 1961.

The Duluth, Missabe & Iron Range Railway was a subsidiary of the U.S. Steel Corporation that hauled iron ore from the Minnesota mines to ports on Lake Superior. The Missabe hauled long, heavy trains and it used huge steam locomotives such as Yellowstone 225 to move its traffic. These engines were the most powerful in the world in terms of tractive effort. I was lucky enough to witness the last Missabe ore train operated with steam in July 1960. A year later two of the line's Yellowstones were fired up to haul a pair of excursion trains on circle trips out of Duluth, Minnesota.

Plate 59 Illinois Central Railroad 4-8-2 2524 at Paducah, Kentucky, February 1960.

In 1959 my friend Don Phillips sent stamped postcards every week to the Illinois Central Railroad roundhouse foremen at Centralia, Illinois, and Paducah, Kentucky, asking if any steam locomotives were in service. Phillips knew that IC had steamers in reserve at both points for use if traffic levels demanded. The Paducah foreman returned a card in February 1960 indicating that twelve engines were in use. Phillips called me, I got on a TWA Super Constellation to St. Louis, and we met in Paducah. We had no car and photographed in the yards and engine terminal, but we did walk to the edge of town to photograph 4-8-2 2524 leaving with a coal train for the power plant at Metropolis, Illinois.

Plate 60 Westbound mixed train runs downhill on the Guayaquil and Quito Railway at Siberia, Ecuador, August 22, 2003.

The extinct volcano Chimborazo is the highest mountain in Ecuador, at more than 20,500 feet. The mountain section of the Guayaquil and Quito Railway climbs from the coast to the 10,648-foot summit of the Palmira Pass. From there to Quito the line is an up-and-down affair with milder grades than on the mountain section. The high point on the railway (11,841 feet) is at Urbina, twenty-six miles north of the city of Riobamba. Urbina lies at the base of Chimborazo and is a cold and windy place. In this photo 2-8-0 53 drifts downgrade, returning to Riobamba from Urbina with a mixed train. The well-known triple peaks of Chimborazo rise up out of the mist.

Plate 61 South African Railways 19D-class 4-8-2 with a westbound special passenger train on the Maclear branch at Glen Wallace, Cape Province, May 28, 1992.

I visited South Africa eleven times between 1965 and 1975 to photograph the railways. By the mid-1970s it was evident that steam was beginning to wind down. I had seen the decline of steam in North America and Europe and didn't want to see it in South Africa. I decided to devote my limited time to photographing in other countries. By the early 1990s steam was almost gone on South African Railways, but a fleet of "Prestige" steam locomotives had been kept to accommodate special trains, and I was persuaded to ride on two of them. A group of seventy to eighty photographers (mostly British, with a few Americans and Germans) rode on a chartered train for about two weeks, sleeping and eating (and drinking) on the train. Numerous locomotives and train consists were available and wonderful locations were chosen for photography. On the 1992 trip the group managed to get 104 photographs in fourteen days. Most of them were good.

Plate 62 Norfolk and Western Railway 4-8-4 611 at Plum Run, Ohio, September 14, 1992.

The Norfolk and Western Railway traversed some rough country in Virginia, West Virginia, and Ohio, and many distinctive steel trestles were part of the line. The Portsmouth to Cincinnati, Ohio, section of the main line was a single track railroad that did not see heavy freight traffic, but it had all of the characteristics of an N&W line, including steel trestles, color position light signals, and N&W's signature pole line, which can be seen under the trestle. In this photograph 4-8-4 611 is westbound, headed for Cincinnati to position itself for excursions the following weekend.

Plate 63 Triple action shot on South African Railways at Bloemfontein, Orange Free State, August 14, 1971.

Just east of Bloemfontein passenger station the Noupoort main line crosses above the Bethlehem line. South African photographer Charlie Lewis, who lived in Bloemfontein, thought that it might be possible to photograph three moving steam trains at this location, and he set about making the necessary arrangements. Charlie worked for SAR and knew everyone. He would begin before dawn, visiting the station-master, yardmaster, and dispatcher and talking with engine crews as they went on duty. Watches had to be synchronized and everyone instructed to watch the movement of the other trains and to make smoke as required. Lewis had tried this shot many times, and often got two trains, but the third was elusive. One Friday night I was having dinner with Charlie and his wife, and the suggestion was made that we try the triple shot in the morning. Arrangements were made and the shot worked! It was my first try.

Plate 64 American-built Liberation 2-8-2s at the French National Railways Nevers roundhouse, January 10, 1968.

French National Railways was formed from nine separate companies in 1938. Prior to World War II France had more than 17,000 steam locomotives. By the time the Allied armies liberated France in late 1944 only 3,000 were operable. In March 1945 a delegation of French railway officials visited the United States and gave specifications for a new 2-8-2 locomotive to design engineers at Baldwin Locomotive Works. SNCF needed these locomotives badly, and construction was spread among the five major North American locomotive builders, who produced 1,340 of these machines in two batches between 1945 and 1947. Only 1,323 of the engines arrived in France. A ship sank in a North Atlantic storm in 1947, taking seventeen locomotives with it. The new 141.R engines were dubbed "Liberation" type and went to work all over France, pulling both freight and passenger trains. Some burned coal and some oil but they were simple, rugged, and dependable. They were among the last steam locomotives operated by the SNCF.

Plate 65 Soviet Railways SU-class 2-6-2 in a blizzard at Matarov, Ukraine, December 10, 1992.

Most of the Ukraine is fairly flat, forested country. In the far southwestern part of the country the Carpathian Mountains add a bit of contour to the countryside. The railway line from Ivano-Frankovsk to Rachov climbs a steep valley and terminates just short of the Romanian border. In this photograph, 2-6-2 SU 251-86 fights heavy snow as it pulls a passenger train on the climb to Rachov. The SU engines were a 1925 design that, in true Soviet fashion, were produced in large numbers until 1951. More than 3,700 of these engines were built, and they were the standard Soviet passenger locomotive for many years.

Plate 66 Mozambique Railways 4-8-2 on the turntable at Lourenço Marques, Mozambique, October 5, 1966.

Caminhos de Ferro de Moçambique operated five disconnected railways inland from Indian Ocean ports. The largest of these systems was centered on Lourenço Marques, the country's largest port. This system connected with South African Railways and Rhodesia Railways and carried heavy traffic. In 1964 a new railway was built across Swaziland to carry iron ore from a mine at Ka Dake to the port for export to Japan. Trains on the 137-mile line were operated under contract by CFM, and twelve heavy 4-8-2 locomotives built in Canada in 1948 were assigned to handle the ore trains.

Plate 67 German Federal Railways class 44 2-10-0 leaves Kassel, West Germany, August 5, 1964.

Kassel was a particularly interesting German city in the early 1960s for a railway photographer. I was drawn there to see the two super-modern class 10 4-6-2s built for Deutsche Bundesbahn, which were in service on express trains between Frankfurt and Kassel. These engines, built by Krupp in 1957, were the world's last new high-speed steam locomotives. Once in Kassel, I discovered a very busy railway center, with main lines radiating in four directions. In this scene at Kassel-Kirchditmold, a suburban station on the edge of the city, a class 44 2-10-0 accelerates a freight train toward Paderborn as a class 41 2-8-2 pauses at the station with a local passenger run bound for Bebra.

Plate 68 A mechanic tightens a pipe joint on a South African Railways locomotive at Bethlehem, Orange Free State, August 18, 1965.

The Nationalist Party took control of the South African government in 1948 and began to impose a system of apartheid. The railways were the largest government-run organization in the country, and job categories were strictly regulated. Jobs reserved for whites included locomotive and train crews, station staff, signalmen, and of course management. But there were plenty of employment opportunities for nonwhite workers on SAR. Many learned skills necessary to advance from manual labor jobs. The difficulty of recruiting white workers for many railway jobs eventually broke down the strict segregation of categories of employment. In this photograph, a mechanic appears to be making an adjustment to auxiliary piping atop the boiler of a 4-8-2. Apartheid was in full bloom at the time but this man was making a living on the railways.

Plate 69 French National Railways 4-8-2 241.P17 at the Le Mans engine terminal, July 7, 1963.

André Chapelon was the chief mechanical engineer of the Compagnie de Paris à Orléans. In the 1930s he redesigned one of the railway's early 4-6-2s and doubled its power output. The locomotive was a four-cylinder compound and Chapelon applied his theories of improved boiler drafting and streamlined steam flow to greatly improve its performance and fuel consumption. After nationalization of the French railways in 1938, Chapelon became chief of locomotive studies for the French National Railways. He designed a number of advanced steam locomotives prior to his retirement in 1953. Engineers in many countries were designing modern steam locomotives during this period, including Woodard and Kiefer in the United States, Stanier, Gresley, and Bulleid in Britain, and Wagner in Germany, but Chapelon is generally regarded as the greatest locomotive design engineer of the twentieth century. Most notable among Chapelon's locomotives were the thirty-five 241.P 4-8-2s produced between 1948 and 1952. I saw them operating out of Le Mans in the early 1960s.

Plate 70 Southern Pacific and Union Pacific 4-8-4s ascend Cajon Pass on parallel tracks at Alray, California, May 8, 1989.

The Los Angeles Union Passenger Terminal was built in 1939. To mark the fiftieth anniversary of the beautiful art deco building the major railroads serving Los Angeles brought historic equipment to the city. Union Pacific ran its 4-8-4 8444 from Cheyenne, Wyoming, for the occasion, and Southern Pacific allowed Doyle McCormack to run down from Portland, Oregon, with Daylight 4-8-4 4449. After the ceremonies were over, both trains were scheduled to run to Portland on their respective railroads. Leaving the Los Angeles basin, trains of both railroads climb through Cajon Pass on separate tracks. The trains were scheduled so as to allow them to ascend the pass in parallel. My good friend David Goodheart produced railroad videos and arranged for a helicopter for his cameraman to shoot the two trains in Cajon. I rode along to take still photographs.

Plate 71 Southbound South African Railways freight train at Toorwater, Cape Province, August 24, 1975.

One of the more impressive locations on the Port Elizabeth–Cape Town railway line is Toorwaterpoort, a steep chasm that provided the only possible route for a railway through the Groot Swartberg Mountains. Toorwaterpoort was located in very desolate country between Klipplaat and Oudtshoorn. A photographer could get fairly close to the south end of the poort on passable dirt roads, but the last few miles involved a hike. Traffic was not heavy but freight trains ran on a fairly predictable schedule, and a walk into the poort could be rewarding.

Plate 72 Three China Rail 2-8-2s move a coal train to Chengde steelworks, January 19, 1995.

Chengde is a small provincial city in China's Hebei Province to the north of the capital, Beijing. In the 1990s most trains on China Rail on the lines radiating out of Chengde were still steam powered. A branch line built to serve a steel mill and power plant at Shuangtashan, fifteen miles from town, included a 3 percent grade on the climb to a summit tunnel. The usual QJ 2-10-2 locomotives used all over China Rail were too heavy for this line, so trains were powered by smaller SY- and JS-class 2-8-2s. They operated three to a train, pulling and pushing in various combinations to get short trains of coal and ore up the hill.

Plate 73 Indonesian State Railways local passenger train at Tjitjapar, Java, September 29, 1971.

Since car rentals were not available in Indonesia in 1971, my companions and I traveled by train, often riding on the locomotives. When an opportunity presented itself, we sometimes hired a taxi to take us to scenic locations in the countryside. In this photograph the afternoon local passenger train is bound from Bandjar on the Bandung–Jogjakarta main line to the town of Tjidjulang, near the Indian Ocean coast. It is pulled by a BB-10 locomotive dating from 1906.

Plate 74 Rebuilt Merchant Navy–class 4-6-2 35003 "Royal Mail" at Basingstoke, England, December 28, 1961.

Southern Railway introduced its Merchant Navy–class 4-6-2s in 1941. Designed by O. V. S. Bulleid, Southern's chief mechanical engineer, these engines introduced a number of novel improvements to British locomotive practice. They were three-cylinder engines with an innovative chain-drive valve gear system, welded boilers and fireboxes, and cast steel drivers. They were covered with an "air-smoothed" boiler casing. Thirty of these engines were built between 1941 and 1949, and all were named for shipping lines calling at Southampton. All thirty of the engines were rebuilt between 1956 and 1959. The complex valve gear was replaced and the air-smoothed boiler casings were removed. These engines served into the mid-1960s.

Plate 75 Double-headed C-62-class Hudsons on Japanese National Railways at Shikaribetsu, Hokkaidō, January 21, 1971.

On my first visit to Japan, in 1966, I met a railway enthusiast named Takao Takada, who was a senior executive at Kisha Seizo Kaisha, Japan's largest locomotive producer. Takada had worked on the team that designed the C-62 4-6-4s, and he was very proud of these engines. Takada showed me photos he had taken of American-built engines running in China. Since China had been closed to foreign travel since the Communists took power in 1949, I asked Mr. Takada how he had obtained them. Takada replied that he had been military governor of Manchuria in 1937 and had taken the photos in his spare time. Takada told me where the C-62s were in service and urged me to photograph Japan's premier passenger locomotives. By 1971 only a few C-62s were still in service, pulling express trains on Japan's northernmost island of Hokkaidō.

Plate 76 Black Five 4-6-0s pass on British Railways at Carlisle, England, August 28, 1964.

Carlisle has always been an important railway junction. Located in northern England just a few miles below the Scottish border, it was the crossroads for railway traffic between the industrial centers of England and Scotland and also lay astride the West Coast main line. Prior to 1923 Carlisle was served by seven separate railway companies. The grouping of railways in 1923 reduced that number to two, with the majority of lines being folded into the London, Midland & Scottish Railway. After the 1948 nationalization of the railways, Carlisle was the break point for operations on three regions of British Railways. Facilities in Carlisle dated from the nineteenth century, with stone and brick bridges and buildings blackened with the soot of the passage of millions of trains over the years.

Plate 77 Three British Railways 2-6-0s around the indoor turntable at York, England, August 29, 1963.

York was an interesting place to photograph British Railways. Located on the East Coast main line 188 miles north of London, the city had been a hub of the London & North Eastern Railway before nationalization in 1948. When I first visited York in 1961 and 1962, operations were predominantly handled by steam locomotives. By 1963 the transition to diesel traction was well under way, but there was still plenty of steam in action on freight and secondary passenger trains. In this photograph, three modern 2-6-0 locomotives await the call to duty. The two engines on the left are K-1-class locomotives designed by LNER but delivered to British Railways after nationalization. Seventy of these engines were built in 1949. The engine on the right is a considerably smaller British Railways standard class 3 mixed traffic 2-6-0, twenty of which were built in 1954.

Plate 78 Southbound National Railways of Mexico freight train near Victor Rosales, Zacatecas, August 17, 1962.

After the major U.S. and Canadian railways dieselized in 1960, National Railways of Mexico continued to operate a major portion of its system with steam locomotives. The arid northern part of the country had been dieselized by this time, but more than four hundred steam engines operated on lines in central and southern Mexico. The northernmost steam operation was on the Central Line to Ciudad Juárez, where steam operated as far north as Felipe Pescador, 504 miles from Mexico City. In this photograph a steam-powered local freight is not far out of Felipe Pescador, bound for Aguascalientes. It is hauling a dead diesel locomotive headed to NdeM's main diesel shop at San Luis Potosí.

Plate 79 Grand Trunk Western Railroad 4-8-4 6325 with a freight train on the Ohio Central Railroad at Morgan Run, Ohio, October 6, 2002.

I met Jerry Joe Jacobson in the late 1950s when we were teenagers photographing the last U.S. steam locomotives. Jacobson trained as a medical professional, and I went on to law school. Jacobson never lost his interest in railroading and ended up in the short line railroad business. He assembled the Ohio Central Railroad System by buying or leasing lines that the major railroads were abandoning and built it into a successful company. Jerry liked steam locomotives, and he purchased several dozen for his private collection. After the Grand Trunk Western dieselized, 4-8-4 6325 was donated to the city of Battle Creek, Michigan, and was on display from 1959 to 1985. Jacobson bought the engine in 1993 and restored it to operating condition in 2001.

Plate 80 New Zealand Government Railways 4-8-4 climbing Cass Bank, South Island, July 21, 1966.

The Southern Alps of New Zealand's South Island include peaks of more than 12,000 feet. The railway from the South Island's major city Christchurch to Greymouth on the Tasman Sea coast crosses the Alps via Arthur's Pass. I first visited New Zealand in 1966. By then steam operations on NZGR were limited to the South Island, and I concentrated my efforts there. The spectacular scenery and winter conditions produced some wonderful photographs, and I returned again in 1967 to catch the last of New Zealand's big engines at work. Here engine 966 hauls a goods train up Cass Bank on its way to Arthur's Pass, where it will hand its train over to electric locomotives. Following a train up Cass Bank was possible on a dirt road that followed the railway line, as the trains did not move too fast. The road ran through sheep paddocks, and the local ranchers expected people using the road to close the fence gates behind them. I got pretty good at opening and closing gates in a hurry.

Plate 81 Nickel Plate Road 2-8-4 759 westbound on Penn Central near Horseshoe Curve, Pennsylvania, September 13, 1970.

The Nickel Plate Road operated a large fleet of modern Berkshire 2-8-4 locomotives. Lima Locomotive Works built 759 in 1944 and it ran in regular freight service until 1959. In 1966 the engine was acquired by the High Iron Company, which had been organized by Ross E. Rowland, a New York commodities trader. The engine was rebuilt in the Nickel Plate roundhouse in Conneaut, Ohio, and I volunteered to assist in the rebuilding effort. As unskilled labor I was given an air grinder and told to remove layers of paint and soot from the engine. It was hot, dirty work but when the engine was first steamed, in August 1968, I was there to record the event. Between 1968 and 1973 the locomotive ran on a series of memorable excursions in the northeastern United States.

Plate 82 Indonesian State Railways mixed train on the high bridge at Lebakdjero, Java, September 26, 1971.

In 1971 I spent five weeks in Indonesia with three other photographers. The trip was planned by Dusty Durrant, a well-known British railway author and photographer. Durrant had been to Indonesia before and had done his homework. We visited the four railways on the island of Sumatra, but most of our time was spent on Java, which had an extensive 3 foot, 6 inch–gauge railway system built during Dutch colonial times. A major objective of the trip was to photograph the scenic line in the mountains east of Bandung, the capital, where large Mallet locomotives were still in use. Here we see a CC-10 2-6-6-0 built in 1904 pulling the afternoon Tjibatu–Tjitjalengka mixed train.

Plate 83 Western Maryland Scenic Railroad 2-8-0 734 westbound at Helmstetter's Curve, Maryland, January 18, 2003.

The Western Maryland Railway's Connellsville Extension was the lowest-grade railroad line across the Allegheny Mountains, with a ruling grade of 1.75 percent. After the 1973 merger of Western Maryland into the Chessie System, traffic was shifted onto the parallel Baltimore & Ohio line, and freight operations ended on the Connellsville line in 1976. The state of Maryland purchased the property and established the Western Maryland Scenic Railroad to operate tourist trains on the fifteen-mile stretch between Cumberland and Frostburg. A highlight of the line is Helmstetter's Curve, a horseshoe of track on a 1.47 percent upgrade that is surrounded by a farm that is owned to this day by the Helmstetter family.

Plate 84 French National Railways Pacific 231.E 624 at Montluçon, January 13, 1968.

It is 1 a.m. on a winter's night in Montluçon, France. Train 2009 has just arrived from Gare de Austerlitz in Paris, carrying through cars for Ussel and Le Mont-Dore, two provincial towns in the mountains of the Massif Central. After a long day of photography I often found night photography a hassle, but I pushed myself because the results were often rewarding. It was easier in the winter since daylight hours were shorter. In France in January the sun goes down by 4 p.m., leaving plenty of time for a good French dinner before the night's shooting.

Plate 85 Soviet Railways class SU passenger locomotive at Kolevka, Ukraine, February 27, 1994.

A dark environment can produce some interesting photographs of steam locomotives. I was riding a passenger train that stopped in a rural siding north of Kiev, waiting for an opposing train. I got off with my camera to survey the situation. It was just after dark and a bit of light remained in the sky to outline the trackside trees. Steam from the pop valves was rising behind the boiler of the locomotive and caught the shaft of light from the headlight. Red signals in the distance added a point of interest to the composition. I "painted" the side of the locomotive with four flashbulbs, then got back on the train. The locomotive is SU 252-86, built by the Sormovo Locomotive Works in 1949.

Plate 86 Pere Marquette Railway 2-8-4 1225 rests at Carland, Michigan, April 21, 2007.

In the 1920s the Pere Marquette Railway became affiliated with a group of eastern railroads under the control of the Van Sweringen brothers of Cleveland, Ohio. The Van Sweringen roads formed an Advisory Mechanical Committee to develop modern locomotives. The result of this work was the "Super Power" 2-8-4, first produced in 1934 and built for a number of railroads over the next fifteen years. Pere Marquette 1225 was built by Lima in 1941 and served in heavy freight service until 1951. It was donated to Michigan State University for display in 1957. In the late 1960s, student members of the Michigan State University Railroad Club began rebuilding 1225 with the goal of restoring it to operating condition. It took more than twenty years of fund-raising and volunteer labor but, in 1990, 1225 steamed again.

Plate 87 Nickel Plate Road Berkshire 765 at Henderson, Michigan, October 11, 2009.

The Fort Wayne Railway Historical Society rebuilt Nickel Plate Road 2-8-4 765 in 1979. The engine was built in 1944 and last ran in freight service in June 1958. It was donated to the city of Fort Wayne, and had been exhibited in Lawton Park since 1963. After rebuilding, the big Berkshire operated on more than 140 excursions on a number of major railroads in the eastern United States between 1979 and 1993, when it required a major overhaul and was taken out of service. The society raised the necessary funds, and volunteers rebuilt the 2-8-4 again in 2001–5. In this photograph 765 is pulling a chartered freight train on a former New York Central Railroad line now operated by the Tuscola and Saginaw Bay Railway.

Plate 88 Chesapeake and Ohio Railway 4-8-4 614 passes the water column at Quinnimont, West Virginia, January 17, 1985.

Although the major U.S. and Canadian railroads had been fully dieselized since 1960, the oil crisis of the late 1970s revived interest in coal as a railroad fuel. American Coal Enterprises was a company formed to explore the feasibility of building a coal-burning locomotive using modern technology. Chessie System agreed to allow tests on its railroad. Privately owned Chesapeake and Ohio 4-8-4 614 was fitted with instrumentation to gather data to assist engineers who were designing the new locomotive. For a month the 614 pulled 6,000-ton coal trains in winter conditions between Hinton and Huntington, West Virginia, on the former C&O main line. Nothing ever came of the ACE project but the tests provided an opportunity for some wonderful winter photography.

Plate 89 Canadian Pacific Railway 4-4-0 29 at St. Lin, Quebec, November 6, 1960.

The American Standard–type 4-4-0 was the universal locomotive on North American railroads in the late nineteenth century. Canadian Pacific Railway 29 was built in 1887, and most engines of this type were scrapped in the 1920s and '30s. Number 29 survived until 1959, with two other 4-4-0s, on a branch line in New Brunswick that had several weight-restricted bridges. After the line was dieselized 29 and its sisters were moved to Montreal, where they pulled several excursion trains in 1959 and 1960. The official last run of a Canadian Pacific Railway steam locomotive took place in November 1960, when 29 pulled an excursion from Montreal to St. Lin, Quebec, to mark the seventy-fifth anniversary of the driving of the last spike of the Canadian Pacific transcontinental line.

Plate 90 Spanish National Railways 240F 2586 entering the tunnel at Torralba, Spain, February 1, 1965.

The Madrid, Zaragoza and Alicante Railway was one of the largest railways in Spain at the time of the formation of the Spanish National Railways (RENFE) in 1941. The Zaragoza to Madrid line crossed the Sierra Ministra by following the canyon of the Rio Jalón for seventeen miles through spectacular scenery to the summit tunnel under the Iberian Continental Divide at Torralba. Standard motive power on this grade in the 1960s were RENFE's squat 240F 4-8-0s, which burned oil. These engines were based on a design introduced on the Andaluces Railway in 1935, and were built for the RENFE up until 1953.

Plate 91 German Federal Railways local passenger train crosses the Rhine River at Köln, West Germany, August 11, 1964.

Germany was an interesting country for a railway photographer to visit in the 1960s. Railway facilities had been extensively damaged during World War II, but by the 1960s most had been repaired. In West Germany, railway management wanted to expand electrification as lines were rebuilt but the power-generating capacity for this did not exist. Instead, a major program was launched to rebuild and modernize prewar steam locomotives. The one new type of locomotive that was built in large numbers was the class 23 2-6-2s, 105 of which were constructed from 1950 to 1959 for use on secondary passenger services. These were the last steam locomotives built for Deutsche Bundesbahn.

Plate 92 Union Pacific Railroad 4-8-4 8444 eastbound at Bitter Creek, Wyoming, August 31, 1968.

Trains magazine editor Jim Wrinn has commented that I like my steam locomotive photographs to look like "the burning of Rome." Although railroad operating officials frowned on heavy smoke, I found that the most dramatic pictures of steam locomotives included copious amounts of black smoke. In 1968 my friend Don Phillips and I were in Colorado photographing freight operations on the Denver and Rio Grande Western narrow-gauge lines. We heard that Union Pacific had scheduled 4-8-4 8444 to pull a special passenger movement from Green River to Cheyenne, Wyoming, the next day and so we made the long overnight drive north. We found the 8444 being fired up for a 4 p.m. departure, and in the next few hours I got three of the best pictures I ever took. We were the only photographers present. Lucky for us!

Plate 93 Canadian National Railways 4-8-4 6218 at Shanty Bay, Ontario, February 18, 1967.

Canadian National Railways was one of the last North American railroads to dieselize, and I was able to see its steam locomotives in action in the late 1950s. When CN ended regular steam operations in the spring of 1960 it retained a number of locomotives for excursion trains. Winter conditions in Ontario provided excellent photographic opportunities, and I often traveled north to photograph these trips. Locomotive 6218 was built by Montreal Locomotive Works in September of 1942, the same month I was born, and it remained in excursion service until 1971.

Plate 94 Denver and Rio Grande Western rotary snowplow at Lobato, New Mexico, May 3, 1993.

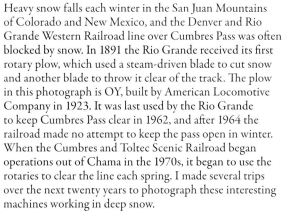

Heavy snow falls each winter in the San Juan Mountains of Colorado and New Mexico, and the Denver and Rio Grande Western Railroad line over Cumbres Pass was often blocked by snow. In 1891 the Rio Grande received its first rotary plow, which used a steam-driven blade to cut snow and another blade to throw it clear of the track. The plow in this photograph is OY, built by American Locomotive Company in 1923. It was last used by the Rio Grande to keep Cumbres Pass clear in 1962, and after 1964 the railroad made no attempt to keep the pass open in winter. When the Cumbres and Toltec Scenic Railroad began operations out of Chama in the 1970s, it began to use the rotaries to clear the line each spring. I made several trips over the next twenty years to photograph these interesting machines working in deep snow.

Plate 95 Fireman wets down the coal on New Zealand Government Railways 4-8-2 1232 at Greymouth, South Island, June 9, 1967.

Preparing a coal-burning steam locomotive for its run is a labor-intensive activity. Coal and water must be loaded into the tender, the fire must be cleaned and raked, and ashes must be dumped from the ash pans. Cinders that have collected in the smoke box have to be shoveled out. All friction bearings on the engine must be lubricated with appropriate grease or oil. If the engine is equipped with a mechanical lubricator, its oil supply must be topped up. In most locomotive depots mechanical staff do this work, but in smaller locations such as Greymouth engine crews often do the work themselves. In this photograph, a J class 4-8-2 is being prepared to take the 7:45 p.m. goods train from Greymouth to Otira, where electric locomotives will take over for the run through the Arthur's Pass tunnel.

Plate 96 South Australian Railways 4-8-4 523 at Mile End locomotive shed in Adelaide, South Australia, August 3, 1966.

South Australian Railways ran an extensive 5 foot, 3 inch–gauge system centered on Adelaide. In the 1920s the railway's Commissioner Webb visited the United States, and upon returning home he announced a plan to "Americanize" the South Australian system. Over the next twenty years a number of classes of heavy locomotives were built to American design standards, culminating in the twelve 4-8-4s of the 520 class produced in 1943 by the railway's own workshop. I had read about South Australia's American-style engines. Unfortunately, I was a bit late in getting to South Australia, since steam operations were winding down quickly. I was lucky enough to find a big 520-class 4-8-4 in steam at Adelaide's Mile End locomotive depot, in reserve in case of a diesel failure on the "Overland" to Melbourne.

Plate 97 Canadian National Railways 4-8-4 6218 at Glanford, Ontario, June 6, 1965.

Canadian National Railway's large fleet of 4-8-4s were fairly light compared to most other North American Northerns and, as a result, were able to run almost anywhere on CN's extensive system. CN ran a program of excursions throughout the 1960s, many of which operated in southern Ontario. These trips were often routed over secondary lines. Here 6218 is hauling a Fort Erie to Paris excursion north toward Hamilton, Ontario, on Canadian National's Hagersville subdivision. The 6218 was the last engine to be overhauled in CN's locomotive shop at Stratford, Ontario.

Plate 98 Soo Line 2-8-2 1003 and 4-6-2 2719 in the rain at Osceola, Wisconsin, August 3, 1998.

Dull weather presents particular challenges for railroad photographers, but once in a while a picture taken under poor conditions works out. I was visiting Osceola, Wisconsin, for a series of charter trains run on the Osceola & St. Croix Valley Railway and the weather was dismal. Steady rain and low light forced me to use a tripod and slow shutter speed, but condensing steam, a bright headlight, and wet concrete resulted in an interesting composition. The locomotives are both of Soo Line heritage, as is the Osceola depot, which is listed on the National Register of Historic Places.

Plate 99 Victorian Railways R-class 4-6-4 at Ararat, Victoria, Australia, August 2, 1966.

In 1966 I went around the world with my good friend Harold Edmonson. Although the primary objective of the trip was to photograph steam locomotives, we both enjoyed riding locomotives, and both tried to ride at least one engine in each country we visited. In August we were in the Australian state of Victoria and encountered one of Victorian Railways' attractive R-class 4-6-4s on a Melbourne–Horsham passenger train. This train made the 203-mile run in five hours and thirty-five minutes. With fourteen intermediate stops (including two fifteen-minute pauses), it really had to move between stations to keep its schedule. It was Edmonson's turn to ride, and I agreed to meet him in Horsham. The train took off out of Ararat like a jackrabbit. I was hard pressed to keep up with it in our rented Volkswagen; I arrived in Horsham some time after the big 4-6-4.

Plate 100 British Railways 35029 "Ellerman Lines" with a London Waterloo–Yeovil express at Basingstoke, England, December 28, 1961.

At Basingstoke, forty-eight miles west of London's Waterloo Station, the Southern Region main line to the south coast cities of Southampton and Bournemouth diverges from the main line to the west of England. In the early 1960s these lines were still steam operated, with Southern Railway's fleet of magnificent Merchant Navy, West Country, and Battle of Britain 4-6-2s pulling most trains. I first visited the Southern Region during the winter of 1961. Days were short and the weather dreary so I took lots of night photographs. One evening I went to Waterloo Station in London for night shots but I was unnerved by the Southern Region's exposed third rail and my metal tripod. The next night I went to Basingstoke, which had no third rail. A constant parade of trains passed through the station, most stopping for two minutes, which was just enough time for a photograph.

Plate 101 A QJ 2-10-2 heads a China Rail passenger train at Shi Nao, January 17, 1995.

I visited Hong Kong on my round-the-world trip in 1966 and rode the Kowloon–Canton Railway up to the border with Communist China. At that time mainland China was closed to Western visitors, and I gazed across the border fence imagining what railway wonders lay on the other side. Fourteen years later, China had opened up to foreign travelers, but travel was restricted to group tours and it was difficult to get out along the railway lines for action photography. I contented myself with photography in engine terminals and in the towns. Another fourteen years and China had truly opened up, and it was possible for photographers to get out to spectacular locations for lineside photographs. Here we see QJ 6091 hauling passenger train no. 453 from Jinzhou in Liaoning Province to Chifeng in Inner Mongolia.

Plate 102 South African Railways passenger train westbound on the Bethlehem–Bloemfontein line at Meynell, Orange Free State, May 25, 1992.

The Bloemfontein to Bethlehem line was a favorite among railway photographers in South Africa. The line skirts the Drakensberg Mountains and runs through some impressive scenery. In the 1960s and '70s motive power on the line was mostly 15-E, 15-F, and 23-class 4-8-2s. In this photograph 4-8-2 3156, built by North British Locomotive Company in 1948, works uphill at Meynell, thirty-eight miles west of Bethlehem. The 3156 was the last built of South African Railways' very successful class 15F 4-8-2s. Between 1938 and 1948, 255 of these engines were built, and they were the mainstay of freight service on many SAR lines.

Plate 103 German Federal Railways freight train crossing the Mosel River at Bullay, West Germany, February 24, 1971.

Deutsche Bundesbahn's Koblenz–Trier line follows the valley of the Mosel River southwest out of Koblenz. At Bullay the river is crossed on a combination rail-highway bridge, after which the line climbs away from the river on its way to Trier. In the early 1970s this scenic line carried heavy freight traffic from the industrial heart of Germany to Luxembourg and France. Standard power on freight trains were class 44 2-10-0s. More than two thousand of these locomotives had been built for Deutsche Reichsbahn and its successor the DB between 1925 and 1949. They were among the last steam locomotives used in West Germany, some remaining in service until 1977.

Plate 104 A French National Railways suburban train leaves Gare St-Lazare in Paris, August 19, 1964.

Big cities were not my favorite places for railroad photography, and I usually avoided them. In 1964 I learned that commuter trains running out of Gare St-Lazare in Paris were still hauled by steam locomotives and I braved the congestion and parking problems to spend a day photographing these trains with urban backgrounds. Movie fans familiar with Jean Renoir's 1938 classic film *La Bête Humaine* may recognize the apartment building in the background as the scene of an assignation between locomotive engineer Jacques Lantier and his murderous lover Séverine.

Plate 105 Medina del Campo station on Spanish National Railways, January 23, 1965.

Medina del Campo was a major junction on the RENFE main line north of Madrid, with lines radiating to cities including Salamanca, Segovia, and Zamora and reaching the Portuguese frontier. The station featured a wrought-iron train shed and wide brick platforms, and it was always busy. Engine 242-0278 is one of sixty mainline tank engines built for the Madrid, Zaragoza and Alicante Railway from 1924 to 1927. The 4-8-4T is pulling through the station to pick up train 1801, bound for Fuentes de Oñoro on the Portuguese border. The crowd on the far platform is awaiting arrival of the "Iberia Express" from Irún on the French border.

Plate 106 Running shed staff prepare Rhodesia Railways 15A-class Garratt 420 for service at Bulawayo, Rhodesia, October 12, 1966.

Rhodesia Railways was an efficient and modern railway that served Southern Rhodesia (now Zimbabwe), Northern Rhodesia (now Zambia), and Bechuanaland (now Botswana). Railways had first reached Rhodesia late in the 1890s as Europeans settled the area. As Rhodesia developed in the first half of the twentieth century the railways were modernized to handle heavy traffic from the copper and coal mines. Modern steam locomotives were purchased, including more than two hundred Beyer-Garratt engines. In this photograph a 4-6-4+4-6-4 Garratt built in France in 1952 is readied for its run at the new (1953) loco shed at Bulawayo.

Plate 107 Coronation 4-6-2 46225 "Duchess of Gloucester" on British Railways at Carlisle, England, January 26, 1964.

I always liked big engines. When I first proposed to visit Britain, my friends derided British locomotives as "tin cans on wheels." Upon my arrival in the UK I found that some of these "tin cans" were formidable engines indeed. Perhaps my favorites were the Coronation-class 4-6-2s, designed by Sir William A. Stanier for the London, Midland & Scottish Railway. First introduced in 1937 as streamlined locomotives, thirty-eight of these impressive four-cylinder machines were built through 1948. The streamlining was later removed, resulting in a very attractive locomotive. The Coronations were all very much in use in the early 1960s on their original assignments, hauling express trains on the West Coast main line between London and Glasgow.

Plate 108 British Railways A-4 Pacific 60010 "Dominion of Canada" at Perth, Scotland, January 31, 1964.

The A-4 Pacifics of the London & North Eastern Railway are among the most famous locomotives in the world. Designed by Sir Nigel Gresley, who was the chief mechanical engineer of LNER from its formation in 1923 until his death in 1941, the locomotives were built for speed. The first of these engines were introduced to pull LNER's early streamlined trains, including "Silver Jubilee," Britain's first streamliner. Thirty-five of these machines were built between 1935 and 1938. One of them, "Mallard," holds the documented world speed record for a steam locomotive at 126 mph, set in 1938. I saw these engines in their original assignment on the East Coast main line as well as in Scotland after they began to be replaced by diesel locomotives on primary trains. The "Dominion of Canada" is seen here about to leave Perth with the 5:30 p.m., ex–Glasgow to Aberdeen express "The Saint Mungo."

Plate 109 An Aberdeen–Manchester fish train pulled by a Britannia 4-6-2 prepares to leave Perth, Scotland, January 30, 1964.

Great Britain has been described by a wag as "a lump of coal surrounded by fish." Both were important to British Railways. The coal, of course, powered the locomotives of Britain's railways, and its increasing price and declining quality had a lot to do with their ultimate demise. The fish were carried on dozens of trains, which operated each night, running between northern ports and the population centers of the Midlands and the south of England. I took lots of night pictures in Britain, and I particularly liked photographing the fish trains in the deserted stations late at night, with just the hiss of steam and the smell of fish and coal smoke.

Plate 110 Norfolk and Western Railway 4-8-4 611 on the bridge westbound at Coopers, West Virginia, October 30, 1982.

After the 1982 merger of Southern Railway and the Norfolk and Western, Southern's steam excursion program continued. Between 1982 and 1994 more than 1,300 trips were operated all over the Norfolk Southern system using eleven different engines. The first big Norfolk and Western engine to return to service was J-class 611, considered by many to be the finest steam passenger locomotive ever built. I had seen and photographed the J's in their last years of regular service, and they were among my favorites. I preferred to see 611 on home Norfolk and Western rails in Virginia, West Virginia, and Ohio, and I made it a point to be there when 611 ran on the old N&W. Fall trips produced the best photographs, with bright sunlight and cold mornings to condense the steam exhaust.

Plate 111 New Zealand Government Railways goods train crossing the Waimakariri River on the South Island, July 21, 1966.

The main attraction of New Zealand's South Island for the railway photographer was not the steam locomotives so much as the surroundings through which they ran. The Midland main line crossed the South Island via Arthur's Pass, linking Christchurch with Greymouth and the coal mining district on the Tasman Sea coast. The line followed the Waimakariri and Broken rivers up to the pass, with snowcapped mountain peaks towering above the tracks on both sides. At Cora Lynn siding the Waimakariri River was crossed on a low steel trestle. In this photograph Ja-class 4-8-2 1242, built in NZGR's own workshops in 1946, takes a westbound goods train across the river as the morning mist lifts from the valley.

Plate 112 Ferrocarriles Argentinos narrow-gauge passenger train at Aguada Troncoso, October 15, 1991.

Patagonia. The very name brings to mind images of treeless plains and plateaus, vast distances, and constant wind. The four southernmost provinces of Argentina constitute Patagonia, and the area is sparsely populated. Early in the twentieth century Argentine State Railways began con-struction of a broad-gauge line meant to open up northern Patagonia to development. This line reached San Carlos de Bariloche, near the Nahuel Huapi National Park, in 1934. To further open up the area, a narrow-gauge branch line was constructed south from Ingeniero Jacobacci (120 miles east of Bariloche) to Esquel. This line, completed in 1945, ran 250 miles through the foothills of the Andes. It was built to 750 mm gauge to cut costs and was operated with a fleet of diminutive locomotives built by Baldwin and Henschel. The barren land never developed much traffic.

Plate 113 Double-headed goods train on New South Wales Government Railways near Amaroo, New South Wales, Australia, May 13, 1967.

In 1967 I spent several months in Australia, where steam was still active in Victoria, Queensland, and New South Wales. On a previous trip I had met a number of Australian railway photographers and would sometimes join these friends on weekend jaunts. A group was planning a trip to western New South Wales and I joined them. The target was a goods train that left Dubbo in the predawn hours, and the group drove to the selected location the night before and camped out. The Aussies were used to camping and had sleeping bags but I had only a light coat, and spent a very uncomfortable night in the backseat of my rented Volkswagen. The hardship was forgotten when the train appeared just before dawn, pulled by one of the big NSW Garratts. At Molong, the train picked up a C-38 4-6-2 to assist it up the twenty-mile grade to Orange.

Plate 114 Canadian Pacific Railway D-10-class 4-6-0 under the coal dock at Vallée Jonction, Quebec, December 31, 1959.

The Quebec Central Railway was a Canadian Pacific subsidiary that ran from Quebec City to Newport, Vermont. Several branch lines were operated out of Vallée Jonction in the French-speaking farm country south of the St. Lawrence River. Quebec Central used Canadian Pacific equipment and was one of the last parts of the CP system to use steam locomotives. CP 1039 has just arrived on the daily mixed train from Lac-Frontière, Quebec. Montreal Locomotive Works built the engine in 1912. It remained in service until the spring of 1960.

Plate 115 Savannah & Atlanta Railway 4-6-2 750 at speed on Seaboard Air Line Railroad tracks near Statham, Georgia, December 3, 1966.

Pacific 750 was built for the Florida East Coast Railway and later sold to the Savannah & Atlanta Railway. After retirement the engine was donated to the Atlanta chapter of the National Railway Historical Society, which operated a number of excursions out of Atlanta, Georgia, in the mid-1960s. She was returning home from an Atlanta–Gainesville–Athens circle trip that ran on Southern Railway and Seaboard Air Line tracks. Highway U.S. 29 paralleled the tracks near Statham and provided an opportunity for me to take several panned photographs from a moving car driven by my friend Don Phillips.

Plate 116 Reading Company 4-8-4 2100 at Drehersville, Pennsylvania, July 4, 1964.

The Reading Company operated a major railroad system centered in eastern Pennsylvania that carried heavy passenger and freight traffic. Reading built thirty modern 4-8-4s in its own shops in 1945. These engines served in freight service until 1956, then were stored at Reading, Pennsylvania. I saw these engines from a passenger train and was intrigued enough by their size to make a trip to look at them up close. I never expected to see one run, but in 1959 Reading began a series of excursions called "Iron Horse Rambles." Over the next five years Reading operated fifty-one trips over its system, using four different 2100s. In this photograph, 2100 is heading a round-trip from Reading to West Milton, Pennsylvania, with American flags on the boiler front to celebrate Independence Day.

Plate 117 British Railways goods train with a banking engine on the rear climbing to Shap summit, at Scout Green, England, August 29, 1964.

As steam locomotives disappeared in Britain in the early 1960s the lines around Carlisle in northwestern England became a focal point of mainline steam operations. The former London, Midland & Scottish Railway main line from London to Glasgow must climb over the Shap summit to reach Carlisle. The summit is only 915 feet above sea level but trains face an arduous climb in both directions. The hills and moors around Shap are home to lots of sheep, and they are often covered with clouds and mist. In this photograph Jubilee-class 4-6-0 45604 "Ceylon" climbs to the summit with a northbound goods train. It is assisted by a 2-6-4 tank engine pushing at the rear.

Plate 118 Japanese National Railways D52-404 southbound along the Hokkaidō coast at Rebun, January 19, 1971.

Many of Japan's railway lines run along the coast, and scenic photographic locations are easy to find. At Rebun, the Muroran main line skirts Uchiura Bay. I found a convenient rock outcropping that allowed the photograph to include waves crashing on the beach and spent several hours photographing freight trains such as this empty coal train hauled by a D-52-class 2-8-2. I suddenly noticed that the incoming tide was cutting off my escape route. A mad dash through the surf resulted in wet feet and frozen pants but I got the shot.

Plate 119 St. Louis–San Francisco Railway 4-8-2 1522 northbound on Wisconsin Central Ltd. rails at Grayslake, Illinois, August 14, 1988.

St. Louis–San Francisco Railway was a major railroad that operated lines in the Midwest and southwestern United States. Its 4-8-2 1522 was built by Baldwin Locomotive Works and operated all over the Frisco system prior to dieselization. The engine ended up in the collection of the Museum of Transport in St. Louis, Missouri. In 1987 the St. Louis Steam Train Association removed the engine from the museum and restored it to operating condition. Over the next fifteen years I saw the 1522 in action all over the former Frisco system. I liked to photograph big engines that had been resurrected when they operated on excursion trains, and I particularly enjoyed seeing 1522 in action because it ran fast and had an extremely loud exhaust when working hard.

Plate 120 Chicago, Burlington & Quincy Railroad 2-8-2 4960 at Ashburn, Missouri, February 19, 1966.

The Burlington Route operated steam locomotives in regular service until 1957 and retained some steamers in reserve after that. A number of these engines were used to power excursion trains, and the Burlington's aggressive Passenger Department cooperated with various railroad clubs and historical societies to run a busy program of special trains between 1958 and 1966. Mikado 4960 was a regular performer on these trips. It is seen here with a train of double-deck commuter cars on a St. Louis to Hannibal, Missouri, round-trip. A cold wind off the Mississippi River condenses the exhaust and leaking steam to create a dramatic scene of winter railroading.

Plate 121 Pusher Locomotive on Denver and Rio Grande Western Railroad narrow-gauge freight train, Lobato, New Mexico, October 12, 1965.

The 4 percent grade on the climb from Chama, New Mexico, to Cumbres Pass limited the load for a K-36 or K-37-class 2-8-2 to about 240 tons. Trains of up to seventy cars were operated on the Rio Grande narrow gauge, and to get a train of this length the fourteen miles from Chama to Cumbres required three trips up the hill. To accomplish this, the railroad operated "Cumbres Turns" of about twenty to twenty-five cars with two locomotives. After the third Cumbres Turn reached the summit of the pass the helper would cut off and the road engine assembled the three pieces of the train to run down the hill to Alamosa. Caboose 0574 was built in 1880 and it is still performing its intended purpose eighty-five years later.

Plate 122 National Railways of Mexico Niagra 4-8-4 with northbound freight train at San Juan del Río, Querétaro, June 7, 1964.

A major attraction of National Railways of Mexico in the 1960s were the 32 class QR-1 4-8-4s (called "Niagras" by the Mexicans), built by Alco and Baldwin in 1946. They were the last U.S.-style 4-8-4s working heavy freight trains in mountainous country. Their home was on the southern portion of the two major trunk lines running north from Mexico City to the U.S. border. About fifty miles north of Mexico City both lines encountered a mountain range that limited a big 4-8-4 to a load of 880 tons northbound and 1,385 tons southbound. A second 4-8-4 was added to heavy trains on the mountain section. In this photograph Niagra 3055 has just dropped its helper after crossing the mountains. The train order signal is set to stop and the crew is in the station picking up orders to continue north.

Plate 123 South African Railways GB-class Garratt on the Barkly East branch in Cape Province, May 26, 1992.

The Barkly East branch ran ninety-seven miles from a junction at Aliwal North in the eastern part of Cape Province. The line skirted the southern part of the Drakensberg Mountains and had numerous grades in excess of 3 percent. In this scene, a mixed train climbs through Motkop to the summit at Drizzly, highest point on the branch, at an elevation of 6,528 feet. The locomotive is a class GB Garratt built in 1921. The seven GBs spent most of their working lives on the Barkly East branch. The GBs were replaced by more modern steam power in 1966, but the 2166, the first of the lot, survived to pull special trains into the 1990s.

Plate 124 Japanese National Railways D-52 2-8-2 with a southbound freight train at Ōnuma, Hokkaidō, June 6, 1966.

The heaviest and most powerful locomotives in Japan were the D-52 2-8-2s, first introduced in 1943. In the early 1950s, 148 of these engines were extensively rebuilt and modernized and they served all over Japan. By 1971 they had been displaced by electrification in most places, but ten were assigned to the Oshamambe terminal in Hokkaidō, where they worked freight trains on the Hakodate and Muroran main lines. In this photograph D52-404 is leaving Ōnuma with a long train of freight cars bound for the ferry terminal at Hakodate, where they will cross the Tsugaru Strait to the main Japanese island of Honshū.

Plate 125 Cuyahoga Valley Scenic Railroad 2-8-2 4070 eastbound on the Pittsburgh & Lake Erie Railroad at Pittsburgh, Pennsylvania, September 28, 1975.

Mikado 4070 was a Grand Trunk Western Railroad 2-8-2 that served in freight service until the end of steam operation in 1960. The engine was bought by a private individual and operated on several trips in the Midwest in the 1960s. Eventually it ended up on the Cuyahoga Valley Scenic Railroad, an excursion operation in the Cleveland, Ohio, area, but occasionally it made trips out of Cleveland. In the fall of 1975, 4070 ventured to Pennsylvania to power an excursion between Pittsburgh and Brownsville. The graceful cantilever signal bridge tells the knowledgeable observer that the Pittsburgh & Lake Erie was once part of the far-flung New York Central System.

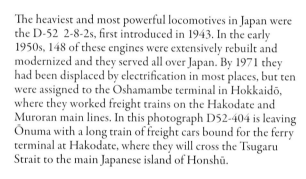

Plate 126 Union Pacific Railroad 4-6-6-4 3985 climbs Sherman Hill in a blizzard at Lynch, Wyoming, October 20, 1984.

Union Pacific crosses the Laramie Range of the Rocky Mountains west of Cheyenne, Wyoming, at Sherman Hill. The builders of the original transcontinental railroad chose this location in 1866 because it was the lowest crossing of the Rocky Mountains possible. Weather on Sherman Hill has always presented the railroad (and photographers) with challenges. The wind always seems to be blowing and heavy snow is common, with drifting in the cuts a major problem. The weather can change quickly, as this photograph attests. The weather was fine when this train left Cheyenne, but twenty-five miles west and a thousand feet higher conditions were quite different.

Plate 127 Union Pacific Railroad 2-8-0 618 along Deer Creek Reservoir at Decker Bay, Utah, March 3, 2002.

The Heber Valley Railroad operates a tourist railroad over sixteen miles of track that once was part of Denver and Rio Grande Western Railroad's Provo Canyon Branch. After the Rio Grande abandoned the branch it was bought by the state of Utah and tourist operations began in 1986. The line is located in a valley in the Wasatch Mountains, surrounded by impressive peaks. When Deer Creek Reservoir was built the railroad was relocated to higher ground along the edge of the water, and there are many excellent photo locations in the area. The Heber Valley has operated a number of different steam locomotives, including engines from Southern Pacific, Great Western Railway, and Union Pacific.

Plate 128 British Railways Castle 4-6-0 at the bumping blocks in Paddington Station, London, December 26, 1961.

Before I went to the United Kingdom in 1961 I had read about the great engineer I. K. Brunel, who built tunnels, bridges, ships, and his greatest accomplishment, the Great Western Railway. I had also seen the photographs of Great Western locomotives taken by the well-known British photographer G. F. Heiron. First stop was of course Paddington Station in London, which at the time was still frequented by British Railways' ex–Great Western locomotives. Number 5057, a four-cylinder Castle class named "Earl Waldegrave," has just arrived with an express from South Wales. This photograph was the first of my pictures to be published, appearing in the April 1963 issue of *Trains* magazine.

Plate 129 Niagra 3054 backs out of National Railways of Mexico's roundhouse at the Valle de Mexico terminal, June 21, 1964.

In the late 1940s and early '50s National Railways of Mexico built a modern freight terminal in the northern suburbs of Mexico City to replace a hodgepodge of older facilities in the city. The complex, near the town of Tlalnepantla, was known as Valle de Mexico. It included a major classification yard opened in 1946 and a thirty-four-stall roundhouse, opened in 1956, the last major roundhouse to be built in North America. In the early 1960s most of the traffic at Valle was still hauled by steam locomotives. In the afternoon conditions were perfect for locomotive photography. I made eight trips to Mexico between 1960 and 1964, and the draw of Valle de Mexico was strong enough that I spent a total of thirty-eight days photographing steam in the area around the terminal.

Plate 130 British Railways interregional passenger train leaves Basingstoke, England, December 28, 1961.

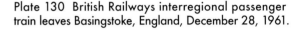

The railway signal, like so many other railway inventions, originated in Great Britain. Fixed signals were in use as early as 1834 in England, and semaphore signals were in use by the 1840s. Two-position semaphores became the standard signals on most British lines, and hand-operated or mechanized versions of these Victorian-era signals were, with few exceptions, still in use everywhere in the 1960s. I often included signals or signal bridges in my photographs. Here we see Western Region engine 5923 "Colston Hall" leaving Basingstoke station on the Southern Region by authority of a lower-quadrant semaphore signal. The train is the 11:05 a.m. ex–Wolverhampton–Bournemouth express.

Plate 131 British Railways goods train with a banking locomotive leaves the yard at Beattock, Scotland, February 4, 1964.

Between Carlisle and Glasgow the former London, Midland & Scottish Railway's London–Glasgow main line climbs to Beattock summit, 1,041 feet above sea level. In the early 1960s the line was extremely busy and still operated for the most part with steam locomotives. At Beattock station heavy goods trains attached a "banking" locomotive on the rear to assist in the ten-mile climb to the summit. In this photograph we see ex-LMS Black Five 4-6-0 44673 leaving the yard at Beattock station with a mineral train, assisted by British Railways standard 2-6-4T 80073. The Black Fives were introduced by the LMS in 1934, and more than eight hundred were built up until 1951. Some lasted in service until the end of steam operations on British Railways in 1968.

Plate 132 Downgrade freight train on Denver and Rio Grande Western Railroad, Los Pinos, Colorado, October 12, 1965.

In their last years of operation the Denver and Rio Grande Western's narrow-gauge freight trains followed a standard operating pattern on a three-day cycle. On the first day trains would start west out of Alamosa and east out of Durango in the morning, then meet in Chama in the evening. On the second day the Durango crew would take the westbound train on to Durango and the Alamosa crew would make two trips up the steep (4 percent) grade with a portion of the eastbound traffic. On the third day the Alamosa crew would take the last of the eastbound cars out of Chama and run to Cumbres, where they would assemble the three parts of the train and continue to Alamosa. In the meantime, the Durango crew would run down the Farmington branch with the cargo destined for that area.

Plate 133 Alberta Prairie Railway 2-8-0 41 at Big Valley, Alberta, May 3, 2006.

Hundreds of towns in the Canadian prairie provinces are dominated by massive grain elevators. These structures were built, mostly in the early years of the twentieth century, as the railways constructed a spiderweb of lines to open the prairies to farming and settlement. By the 1980s major changes had occurred in the way grain was grown, transported, and marketed. The network of lines that served many of the country elevators began to be abandoned by the major railways. Central Western Railway took over operation of Canadian National's Stettler subdivision in 1986 to provide local service. Steam excursions were also operated, using a small 2-8-0 built for a predecessor of the St. Louis–San Francisco Railway and operated by the Mississippian Railway for many years as its number 77.

Plate 134 Guatemalan Railways 2-8-0 at Los Encuentros, Guatemala, December 2, 1977.

The International Railways of Central America was a subsidiary of the United Fruit Company that operated an extensive three-foot-gauge railway system in Guatemala and El Salvador to move the products of the United Fruit banana plantations. The Guatemalan lines were taken over by the government after United Fruit abandoned the system. The main line between Puerto Barrios and Guatemala City traversed some rough country on its 6,000-foot climb from the coast. In this photograph a mixed train on the ninety-four-mile run from Zacapa to Guatemala City runs along a narrow shelf cut from the cliffs. The locomotive is a 2-8-2 of American design but built in Germany by Krupp in 1938. The engines were received as barter for Guatemalan coffee.

Plate 135 Pakistan Railways passenger train climbs the Khyber Pass at Ali Masjid, February 11, 1994.

The British built a railway from Peshawar to the top of the famed Khyber Pass at Landi Kotal to move troops to defend the border between British India and Afghanistan. The line was heavily fortified. After the partition of India in 1947 the railway was operated by Pakistan Railways. It runs through the "Federally Administered Tribal Areas," which means that the Pakistani government does not control this part of the country. Besides the local tribesmen, the area today is home to a huge number of refugees from the wars in Afghanistan. Troops are still stationed here to ensure the security of the railway and the highway in the Khyber Pass.

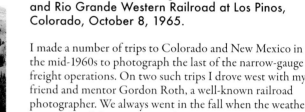
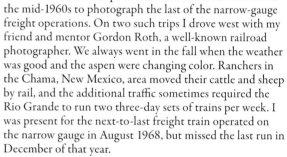

Plate 136 Eastbound freight train on Denver and Rio Grande Western Railroad at Los Pinos, Colorado, October 8, 1965.

I made a number of trips to Colorado and New Mexico in the mid-1960s to photograph the last of the narrow-gauge freight operations. On two such trips I drove west with my friend and mentor Gordon Roth, a well-known railroad photographer. We always went in the fall when the weather was good and the aspen were changing color. Ranchers in the Chama, New Mexico, area moved their cattle and sheep by rail, and the additional traffic sometimes required the Rio Grande to run two three-day sets of trains per week. I was present for the next-to-last freight train operated on the narrow gauge in August 1968, but missed the last run in December of that year.

Plate 137 Soviet Railways freight train in the snow at Malinitci, Ukraine, February 22, 1994.

The 1959 Russian movie *Ballad of a Soldier* tells the story of a young soldier during World War II who is rewarded for his bravery with a furlough to visit his aging mother. To get home he must ride a succession of trains, all steam powered. I saw this movie while I was in college and still remember the many scenes of Soviet steam locomotives running through snow-covered birch forests. I wanted to see and photograph Soviet Railways but did not do so until the country opened up to Western travelers thirty years later, after the disintegration of the Soviet Union.

Plate 138 British Railways 72007 "Clan Mackintosh" leaves Perth, Scotland, with a fish train for London, August 26, 1964.

Perth was a railway center in eastern Scotland that I first visited in 1964. I read that some of the famous A-4 Pacifics had been sent to the Scottish region to work express trains between Glasgow and Aberdeen. Perth had plenty of action, and besides the A-4s there were locomotives from the former London & North Eastern Railway, the London, Midland & Scottish Railway, and the standard British Railway classes introduced after nationalization in 1948.

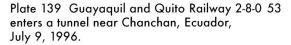

Plate 139 Guayaquil and Quito Railway 2-8-0 53 enters a tunnel near Chanchan, Ecuador, July 9, 1996.

The Guayaquil and Quito Railway climbs from sea level to an Andean summit of 11,841 feet in 170 miles, with grades as steep as 5.5 percent. Things are pretty relaxed in Ecuador, and it is possible to do things that would be considered unsafe anywhere else in the world. Engineer Washington Eloy Alfaro enjoys showing off his locomotive and was amenable to following closely a gasoline railbus up the canyon of the Chanchan River. My fellow photographers and I rode on the roof of the railbus, and Washington followed about a hundred feet behind, running his engine flat out with a short freight train. This sounds dangerous but on the 5.5 percent upgrade Washington could stop his train almost instantly if something went wrong. I rode on the railbus roof the nine miles from Huigra to Sibambe, and the sight and sound of the close-up view of the hard-working locomotive was unforgettable.

Plate 140 South African Railways 15E-class 4-8-2 2939 awaits an evening departure from Bethlehem, Orange Free State, August 18, 1965.

On my first trip to South Africa in 1965 I traveled mainly by rail. South African Railways had a fleet of long-distance passenger trains that served all parts of the country. The trains were old-fashioned but they had comfortable sleeping accommodations, and most carried dining cars that served good food. My journey took me on a four-thousand-mile circle of southern Africa. Early in the trip I stopped for a day in Bethlehem, a railway center in the eastern part of the Orange Free State. Trains at Bethlehem were 100 percent steam operated, and I spent a fruitful day around the yards and locomotive shed. In the evening I photographed a 15E preparing to take train 724 to Kroonstad, and fifteen minutes later I boarded a train for the overnight journey to Bloemfontein.

Plate 141 National Railways of Colombia 2-8-0 at Bogotá, March 19, 1966.

I made one trip to Colombia, in 1966, to photograph that country's system of three-foot-gauge railways. Steam was active on most of the system, and I visited the locomotive shops at Flandes and the railway centers of Espinal and Cali. The trip ended abruptly after eight days when I was thrown by a bull. My injuries were not life threatening and I elected to head to the airport for a flight to New York rather than to a local hospital. I arrived in New York the next morning looking rather bedraggled, which attracted the attention of U.S. Customs agents—who found no contraband—and I went to see my doctor and received a few stitches as well as a battery of antibiotic shots.

Plate 142 British Railways luxury train "The Queen of Scots" leaves Edinburgh Waverley Station for London, January 1, 1962.

"The Queen of Scots" was a Pullman Limited train operated by British Railways with cars owned and staffed by the Pullman Car Company. It ran between Glasgow and London's King's Cross Station via Edinburgh, Newcastle, and Leeds, on a schedule of more than nine hours. The fastest Glasgow to London trains made the run in a little more than seven hours via the West Coast main line. The train did not carry a dining car. Instead, meals and drinks were served to passengers at their seats. In this photograph it is hauled by a modern A-1 Pacific dating from 1948. It may not have been the fastest way to get from Glasgow to London but it was certainly the most comfortable.

Plate 143 An ancient shop engine rides the turntable at the Spanish National Railways locomotive depot at Valladolid, January 24, 1965.

The Spanish National Railways (RENFE) had a tremendous variety of steam motive power in operation in the 1960s. The railways in Spain were badly damaged during the 1936–39 civil war, and once the Franco regime took power the country did not have the funds to fully rehabilitate the railway system. As a result, one could see hundred-year-old locomotives working alongside more modern engines, and most of the stations and support facilities were old. Valladolid was a major railway center on the former Northern Railway line between Madrid and the French border at Irún. There were two turntables and two old roundhouses filled with all kinds of locomotives from the constituent companies that became part of RENFE. Some of the engines in the background of this photo date to the 1920s and '30s. A few modern 141Fs are also present.

Plate 144 Denver and Rio Grande Western narrow-gauge locomotives 487 and 483 lay over at Chama, New Mexico, engine house, October 11, 1965.

The Rio Grande narrow-gauge locomotive facilities at Chama, New Mexico, were like a working museum. The two-stall brick engine house and shop building was all that remained of a nine-stall roundhouse dating from the construction of the railroad in 1880. The Chama engine house provided an interesting background for night photographs of the Rio Grande's narrow-gauge Mikados. Here we see engine 487, which had arrived from Alamosa that afternoon, and 483, in from Durango. The next day 483 made two runs from Chama to Cumbres up the 4 percent grade, while 487 continued on to Durango. Both locomotives are K-36-class 2-8-2s built by Baldwin Locomotive Works in 1925.

Acknowledgments

A NUMBER OF PEOPLE HAVE ENCOURAGED ME and assisted in producing my railway photographs. The late David P. Morgan, editor of *Trains* magazine for many years, published my work and offered advice that improved my early work. Later editors of *Trains,* including Kevin Keefe and Jim Wrinn, continued to support my efforts.

My good friends Gordon Roth and Ronald Wright taught me many of the photographic skills that I had to learn to do a competent job. Many lifelong friends were traveling companions who shared my adventures and took photographs (or just watched trains) alongside me over the years, including Don Phillips, Harold Edmonson, Mike Eagleson, Charlie Lewis, Greg Triplett, the late David Goodheart, Bill Botkin, Jim Thomas, Howard Fine, Nils Huxtable, and Rick Ahearn. We had some good times on those trips.

My mother, Angela Hand, encouraged my railroad interest from an early age. My father, Morton Hand, taught me the basics of photography and, despite his misgivings at first, finally accepted my compulsion and appreciated my railroad photography.

This book would not have been created without the interest and support of Wendy Burton and Jeff Brouws and the editorial and marketing staffs at W. W. Norton, including Jim Mairs, Austin O'Driscoll, and Bill Rusin.

Finally, I must acknowledge the support of my wife, Patricia, who encouraged (and put up with) my all-consuming avocation during forty years of marriage. My friends call her Saint Pat.

Victor Hand
Bar Harbor, Maine
February 2013